A Pattern Book of

Tatting

Mary Konior

B.T. Batsford Ltd · London

First published 1985
Reprinted 1988, 1992
© Mary Konior 1985, 1988, 1992

Printed in Great Britain
by Courier International, East Kilbride, Scotland

Published by
B.T. Batsford Ltd
4 Fitzhardinge Street
London W1H 0AH

A catalogue record for this book is available from the British Library.

ISBN 0 7134 6537 9

Acknowledgements

With grateful thanks

to Patricia Knowlden, who once taught me to tat and is unwittingly responsible for this book
to the West Kent Federation of Women's Institutes, who encouraged me to teach
and to the Ring of Tatters, whose appetite for new patterns is insatiable

Contents

Introduction   4

1 Equipment for Tatting   7
2 How to Tat   10
3 Special Techniques   16
4 The Patterns   21
   Edgings
   Braids and Strips
   Composite Laces
   Individual Laces and Fragments
5 How to Use Tatting   88

Appendix   92
Bibliography   93
Suppliers   95
Index   96

Introduction

Shuttle lace, better known by its unbeguiling name of tatting, has a tracery of thread and form which is fascinating. Many have fallen for its charm.

The shuttle provides a means for knotting thread in such a manner that the resultant lace forms in one's hands. Fingers with a light touch, worthy of a practising pickpocket, are thus a desirable asset, and much of the enchantment of the work is due to the finger play involved in knotting the thread—play akin to the cat's cradle games of childhood. At first sight the knot seems simple enough, but the process of tatting is not all that it appears to be, for the active thread which cavorts around does not itself form the knot but is an agent which manipulates a passive secondary thread into knot form. The knot is a reversed double half-hitch, usually called a double stitch in tatting patterns.

Historically, tatting is a development of an earlier practice known as knotting, which featured in early embroideries. A heavy thread or cord, knotted at close intervals like a string of beads, would be couched to fabric to outline a design or laid *en masse* as a filling, knots of varying size and complexity resulting in different textures. During the late-seventeenth and eighteenth centuries, a fashion for knotting for the purposes of embroidery swept through the ladies of Western Europe and, although very few of the ensuing embroideries have survived, there are numerous literary references to the work in contemporary diaries, letters and verse, plus pictorial evidence in paintings. Many examples of ornate knotting shuttles are still in existence. These are larger than tatting shuttles, being designed to accommodate the thicker threads of their day.

The transition from knotting to tatting was a gradual process difficult to date. At some stage the half-hitches multiplied excessively, causing the knots to expand into ring formation, and at a further stage the rings acquired picots and became sufficiently attractive in their own right to be freed from the confines of embroidery and joined together to make a lace fabric.

A mass of small rings awaiting assembly into lace must often have seemed a disastrous tangle of knots, and possibly this accounts for the name, tatting. 'Tat' was an old expression, of Icelandic derivation, common in northern dialects, for a tangled knot in wool or hair. Catherine Cookson, in her novel *The Whip* (William Heinemann, 1983), set in nineteenth-century County Durham, writes, 'The combing wasn't gentle but it wasn't rough because when her granny came to a tat she held the upper part of her hair in her hand while she combed through it.'

The first tatted laces were concentric rounds of ringlets bedizened with picots and suggestive of the hedgerow florets of 'Queen Anne's lace'. A tattered example, typical of tatting at the beginning of the nineteenth century is shown below. It was made as a series of tiny rings which were afterwards sewn into circles with a thread taken across the back of the work, the surfeit of picots serving to camouflage signs of sewing. The resultant pieces were then tied individually.

Since a needle was in use to assemble the component rings, needlepoint lace fillings were commonly added to the open centres of tatted circles. Sometimes too, a needle was used to overcast any

An early example of tatting, circa 1820

threads which led from ring to ring, so forming needlepoint bars or chains. Tatted chains, made with a shuttle, were a Victorian development, dating from 1864, and usually attributed to Eleonore Riego, a famed needlewoman and designer of her day. The present method of joining rings with a shuttle was first published in 1851. These two important improvements to tatting set the traditions for the beautiful craft that it became during the following decades and during its glorious Edwardian heyday. One technique which has survived intact from the earlier knotting and is still in use now, is the Josephine knot, presumably named, or more correctly re-named, after Empress Josephine.

Published directions began to be generally available in the late-Victorian and Edwardian eras, and many favourite patterns of today can be traced to these sources. Some of the early publications, and details of books giving a more comprehensive account of the history of tatting, are listed in the Bibliography.

The practice of naming designs is a common indulgence. This collection takes its inspiration from plant form or from nursery and folklore, on the assumption that the latter may well be of an age comparable with the evolution of tatting. Also it adds amusement and aids concentration when following a pattern such as 'Oranges and Lemons' to know whether the ring that one is in the process of working is an Orange or a Lemon!

Tatting can be exquisitely delicate or heavily bold, depending on the thread selected. Many of the designs shown are enlarged for clarity of illustration, and are more dainty in actuality than is apparent. Much of the allure of tatting depends on its openwork peek-a-boo quality, and the spaces or negative areas in a design are of as much aesthetic importance as the solid forms of the knots. Despite the open character of the work, tatting is one of the toughest of laces when well made, and it holds its shape well. However, it is not so much for its strength that tatting is loved by its devotees as for its engagingly frivolous prettiness.

Shuttle lace, or tatting, is also known by its French name of *frivolité* and by its Italian names of *occhi* (which means 'eyes') and *chiacchierino* (which means 'chatter' or 'tattle'), the latter providing an alternative clue, or red herring, to the English name. Its German name is *Schiffchenspitze* (which means 'shuttle lace'), and many other languages use their own terminology for this description.

1 Equipment for Tatting

Shuttles

Traditional shuttles are quite small, usually 6 cm to 7 cm in length, this being an optimum size for working at speed. Too large a shuttle can be cumbersome and can inhibit an even rhythm of work. The traditional simple shuttle has points at each end which just meet but are sufficiently flexible for easy winding. The test of a simple shuttle is that it should hold its thread and not unwind if it suffers from falling sickness and is accidentally dropped.

Models of a more sophisticated design have a central spool which can be removed for winding. A small hook is a necessary adjunct for tatting, and for this reason some shuttles have a hook incorporated into their design and set at one of the points, thus negating the need for a separate hook.

Antique shuttles are often exquisite and covetable. Bone and tortoiseshell were commonly used for simple shuttles, but ivory, mother-of-pearl, veneered and lacquered woods, and all sorts of precious and semi-precious materials were employed for the purpose. The carved ivory shuttle on page 8 is Chinese, although it must have been intended as an ornamental accessory for a workbox rather than as a working shuttle. It is almost impossible to use, since the thread continually catches on the carving.

Tatting hooks

A small hook can sometimes be purchased with the shuttle. A tatting hook is shorter than a crochet hook and formerly it was attached to a thumb ring worn on the left hand. The thumb ring is now obsolete, but a tatting hook can be threaded on ribbon and worn around the neck or wrist. A steel crochet hook of size 1.50 mm or smaller makes a good substitute.

Threads

Mercerized crochet cottons are excellent for tatting, being smooth and strong. The thickest crochet cotton that a simple shuttle will

accept is usually No. 10, and the finest available crochet cotton, No. 150, is only just strong enough for use.

Opposite: Shuttles, old and new

The size of thread for each pattern is given solely as a guide; there is no reason why different sizes should not be used, nor is it essential to keep to crochet cottons. Sewing cottons, silk or polyester top-stitching threads, and many embroidery threads are all feasible, although stitches will glide more quickly and neatly into place with a mercerized or silk thread than with a matt thread. The thread chosen needs to be sufficiently strong to withstand the pull of a shuttle without snapping, and sufficiently hardwearing to last the intended life span of any article to which it will be attached.

To fill a simple shuttle, tie the thread to its centre and wind as much as the shuttle will conveniently hold without thread protruding beyond the sides, where it would easily soil. Hands should be immaculately clean, as it is important to keep threads in pristine condition during work. A removable central spool can often be fitted to a sewing machine for fast winding.

Other equipment

Scissors, pins and needles are also needed for tatting.

2 How to Tat

There are two basic methods of tatting, both well known since mid-Victorian times, although there are several minor variations of each. The basic methods refer to the manner of passing the shuttle in order to form a preliminary half-hitch. The process by which this half-hitch on the shuttle thread is subsequently transferred to the passive secondary thread is common to all methods, and it is this latter process which often presents problems to a beginner, especially if hands are gnarled by hard work. Annoyingly, an eager child can often acquire the knack at about the age of seven.

To understand this process, try the following experiment.

Take two lengths of string or coarse thread, smooth of surface and of different colours. Knot the two together and use thread B to form a half-hitch or loop on thread A (Fig. 1(a)). Grip the knot with the left hand and tug thread B sharply. The loop on thread B should transfer to thread A, and the original half-hitch has now become a half-stitch in tatting (Fig. 1(b)). In practice, thread B is wound on the shuttle and thread A is the thread from the ball or whatever source. Half-stitches are worked in pairs to form the double stitch which is the basis of all tatting.

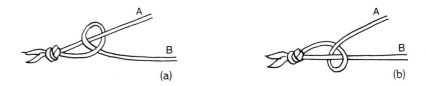

Fig. 1 Transfer of the half-hitch

Method 1

To make a chain of double stitches
Using two threads of different colours, wind the shuttle with B and leave A running from the ball. Knot both together, grip the knot in the left hand with the thumb and first finger, and take the ball thread

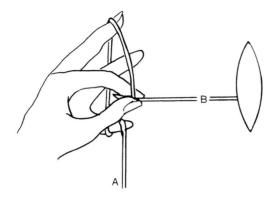

Fig. 2 Holding the threads to make a chain

A over the back of the outstretched fingers and around the fourth finger (Fig. 2). Place shuttle thread B in a loop over the top of the left hand and pass the shuttle upwards, under A and through the loop made by B (Fig. 3(a)). This will result in thread B looped on thread A as shown in Fig. 1(a). Transfer the loop to thread A, as shown in Fig. 1(b), with a sharp tug of the shuttle. It is essential that thread A is sufficiently slack to allow this, and the outstretched second finger should be dropped in order to slacken it. The transferred loop is now the first half-stitch. Slide it up next to the knot by gradually stretching the second finger outwards again (Fig. 3(b)). Hold the first half-stitch in position with the thumb.

Fig. 3 Making a first half-stitch

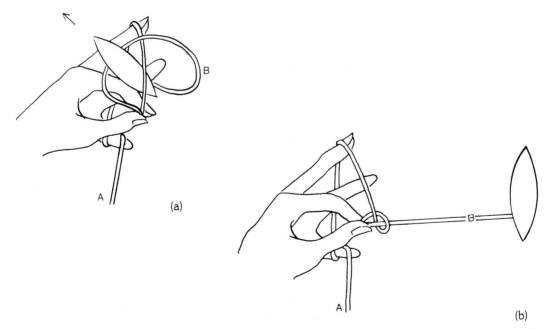

(a)

(b)

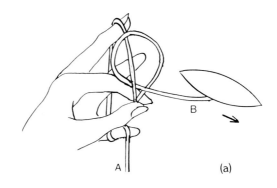

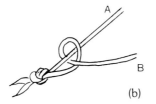

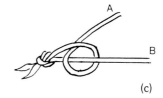

Fig. 4 Making a second half-stitch

To make the second half-stitch, pass the shuttle downwards under A and over B (Fig. 4(a)). This will result in thread B looped on thread A (Fig. 4(b)). Note that the loop faces the opposite way to that shown in Fig. 1(a). Transfer this loop on thread B to thread A as before (Fig. 4(c)). The transferred loop is now the second half-stitch. Slide it up next to the first half-stitch, and note that one is the reverse of the other. Both together form the double stitch (Fig. 5).

Practise a series of double stitches, thus forming a chain. All stitches should slide easily on shuttle thread B.

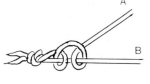

Fig. 5 A double stitch

To make a picot
Leave a small space between stitches, the length of the space depending on the thickness of the thread used. When the stitches are pushed up together, the space forms a picot (Fig. 6).

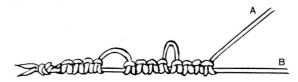

Fig. 6 Making a picot

To make a ring
The shuttle thread is used alone to make a ring. Abandon the ball thread, allowing it to hang loose, and wrap the shuttle thread completely around the outstretched fingers of the left hand to form a ring, gripping it together with the thumb and first finger (Fig. 7). Work a

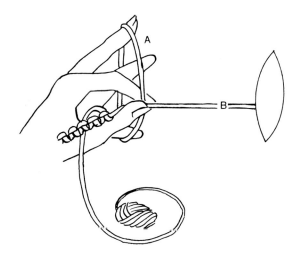

Fig. 7 Holding the thread to start a ring

series of double stitches as shown for making a chain, although A and B are now different parts of the same thread. The ring thread A will gradually become smaller as work progresses, and the outstretched fingers of the left hand will be forced to contract. To enlarge the ring, stretch the fingers out again, still gripping with the thumb and first finger, so that extra thread is fed through to the ring. It is essential that all the double stitches should slide easily on thread B and, if they do not, it means that they have been incorrectly worked at some point, and that the transfer stages shown in Fig. 1(b) and Fig. 4(c) have been omitted. Mistakes can be unpicked with a hook or with a pin, but tatting will not unravel.

To complete and close the ring, slip it off the outstretched fingers, still gripping with the first finger and thumb, and gently pull the shuttle. The ring will close completely, provided that all double stitches are correctly worked (Fig. 8).

To construct a design

Fig. 8 A closed ring

Tatted laces may consist of all rings, or of all chains, but most designs are a combination of both. If, after working a ring, pattern directions then require a chain, pick up the ball thread on the left hand and use both ball and shuttle threads. If, after working a chain, pattern directions then require a ring, drop the ball thread and take the shuttle thread on the left hand. When changing from rings to chains, and vice versa, begin each as closely to its predecessor as possible without leaving any thread or space between them. If a space is required, pattern directions will specify the exact amount. Similarly, when working a series of rings, do not leave a space between each unless this is specified. Usually, work is reversed each time that it changes from ring to chain, and vice versa, and this means turning the ring or chain just completed upside down before starting the next. Directions to reverse work will be given in the pattern.

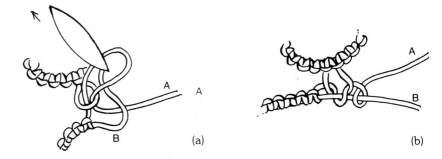

Fig. 9 Joining tatting

To join component parts

Rings and chains are joined to each other by the use of picots, and the method of joining is the same whether working a ring or chain. Insert the hook into a previously worked picot and catch thread A, pulling it out into a loop. Pass the shuttle through this loop (Fig. 9(a)). Tighten and position the loop so that it slides on thread B. The join is counted as a first half-stitch and is followd by a second half-stitch to complete it (Fig. 9(b)). This method of joining, using thread A, is the usual method of joining tatting.

Sometimes, a design will require the shuttle thread to be tied as a join, but this is unusual and will be specified in the pattern. For a shuttle thread join, insert the hook into a ready-made picot, catch the shuttle thread B and pull it out into a loop. Pass the shuttle through and tighten the resultant knot. It is a fixed knot which does not slide, and it does not count as a stitch (Fig. 10).

Fig. 10 A shuttle thread join

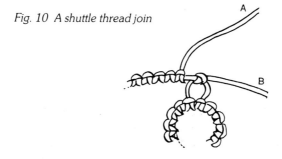

To ensure a good tension

Tatting should be firmly worked and should not be a lank cobweb. Close each ring well, and tighten each chain after it is worked by pushing the stitches well up together, although do not tighten tatting so much that shapes become distorted. Picots required for joins can be made smaller than ornamental picots as they need to be only large enough for insertion of the hook. Eliminate unwanted spaces between rings and chains by being very careful with the position of the first half-stitch at the beginning of each ring or chain.

Method 2

This is a quicker method of working which with practice can become very speedy. However, it is difficult for a beginner to master and, for this reason, it is better to learn using method 1 and to advance to method 2 later.

The differences are in Fig. 3(a) and Fig. 4(a) only, i.e. in the manner of passing the shuttle to make the preliminary half-hitch; all other processes are the same. The way in which the shuttle is held is important. Hold it with the thread leading from the back, using the thumb and first finger of the right hand (Fig. 11). Take shuttle thread B between the third and fourth fingers of the right hand, so that it catches on the tip of the fourth finger, keeping it taut. Pass the shuttle under B and under A, pushing it upwards against A which is also taut (Fig. 12(a)). Keeping the same grip on the shuttle, take it backwards under thread B. The tension of the pushing action should slip thread A over the top of the shuttle and back underneath in one movement, all without the finger and thumb being removed from the shuttle (Fig. 12(b)). At the same time, allow B to drop from the fourth finger and then from the rest of the hand. Thread B is now looped on thread A as in Fig. 1(a), ready to be transferred in the usual way to form a first half-stitch.

Fig. 11 Holding the shuttle

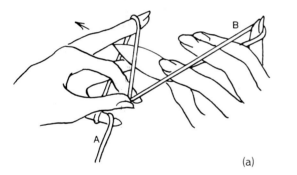
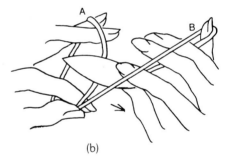

(a)   (b)

Fig. 12 Making a first half-stitch

For the second half-stitch, pass the shuttle to the left, pressing it on top of thread A, which should be taut (Fig. 13). Pressure from the shuttle should cause thread A, underneath, to slip back over the top of the shuttle in one movement, without either finger or thumb being removed from the shuttle. Thread B is now looped on thread A as shown in Fig. 4(b), ready to be transferred in the usual way to form a second half-stitch.

Fig. 13 Making a second half-stitch

15

3 Special Techniques

These are suggestions for improving workmanship once the basics of tatting have been mastered.

To start without a knot

When first winding the shuttle there is no need to sever the thread from shuttle to ball, only to tie the ends together again. However, if making a fresh start and the ball and shuttle threads are already cut asunder, a length can be unwound from the shuttle and wound back on to the ball. Start as usual and, when the break in the ball thread is later reached, work an overlapped join.

To work an overlapped join

Fig. 14 An overlapped join

This method can be used to join on a new shuttle thread or a new ball thread, and it is best worked at the commencement of a ring or a chain. When working a ring, overlap the old and new shuttle threads so that both encircle the hand, clutching tightly. Work the first three or four double stitches, then drop the old thread from the fingers and continue the ring with the new (Fig. 14).

Ends can be clipped once the ring is closed. When working a chain, overlap the old and new threads sufficiently to wrap over the left hand and around the fourth finger, again clutching tightly.

The method gives a slight thickening where the thread is double; so, to compensate for this, fewer stitches need to be worked than given in the pattern. Plan the join so that picots are not worked with the double thread.

To cover the ends of a knot

If there is insufficient old thread left for an overlapped join, or if for any reason threads need to be tied together, the two ends can be hidden by running them with the shuttle thread, inside a few double stitches, as the latter are worked (Fig. 15). This can be done at the beginning of either a ring or a chain and is achieved by using the hook to pull the ends through each half-stitch before each is positioned and tightened.

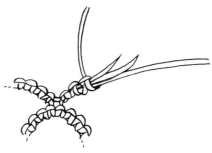

Fig. 15 Covering the ends of a knot

The method is extremely neat, especially if the ends are clipped at different lengths. A further refinement is to lay the ends in opposite directions and to run one into a ring and the other into a chain, although of course this is twice as much work.

To join the first and last rings of a rosette

This is a problem which puzzles many tatters, as the final joining picot so often becomes twisted. Hold the work as shown, the last ring upright and incomplete in the hand, and the first ring to the right (Fig. 16(a)). Fold the first ring forwards to the left, so that the back of it is facing (Fig. 16(b)). Give the joining picot, which will usually be the first picot of the first ring, a half-twist backwards and upwards (Fig. 16(c). Insert the hook from the front in the usual way, complete the join and finish the ring in the usual way. The result should be a perfect join without any unwanted twist. This method is often useful for other difficult joins at the end of a round.

Fig. 16 Joining a rosette

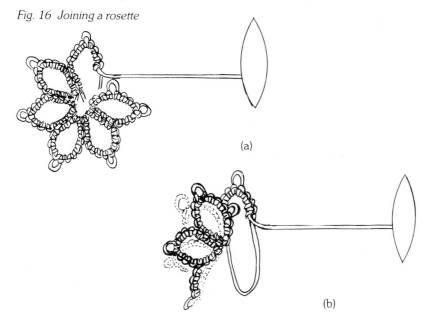

(a)

(b)

(c)

17

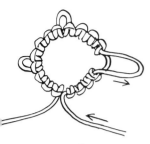

Fig. 17 Opening a closed ring

To open a closed ring

Once a ring is closed, any attempt to open it again by pulling at its base will only tighten the last stitch, so making the task impossible. However, it is often possible to open a ring by easing the stitches apart at some other part of its circumference, preferably beyond half-way round, at a picot, and gently pulling with a hook the running thread there revealed (Fig. 17). Pull gently, concentrating on the stitches to the right of the thread, as a pull to the left will tend to tighten the important last stitch. Once sufficient thread has been loosened, the stitches to the left can be shunted along until the loosened thread appears at the base of the ring, which can then be opened fully and placed back on the hand. Stitches can thus be unpicked as required.

To work a Josephine knot

Work a tiny ring using a series of half-stitches instead of the usual double stitches. Either the first half-stitch or the second half-stitch can be used, but it is essential to keep to the same half-stitch throughout. The second half-stitch is usually quicker to work.

Josephine knots are sometimes featured in all-ring designs, positioned on the space threads which link the rings. On chain designs, they are sometimes positioned on the chains, like picots. In this case, the Josephine knots are worked with the ball thread, which is wound on a second shuttle for the purpose. The need for a second shuttle will always be specified in a pattern.

To use two shuttles

When the ball thread is wound on a second shuttle, the main shuttle is held in the right hand and the thread from the second shuttle is held on the left hand in the same way as the thread from a ball. To change shuttles, hold the second shuttle in the right hand, and either drop the main shuttle (when making a ring or Josephine knot) or use the main shuttle on the left hand (when making a chain).

To add beads to tatting

The most practical way to bead tatting is to thread the beads on the ball thread before starting work. Each bead is then slipped up into position on a chain when required. Small beads look well positioned on picots (Fig. 18(a)) or placed between chains (Fig. 18(b)). If beads

Fig. 18 Adding beads to chains

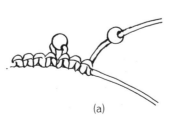

(a)

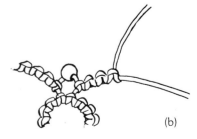

(b)

of different types are used, any relevant sequence should be planned in advance, and the beads threaded in reverse order of use. It is not usually convenient to thread beads on the shuttle thread as they will impede work, but beads can be added to all-ring designs if each is slipped onto a joining picot just before the join is made. Each picot must be long enough to take the hook after the bead is added. A short length of fine wire will make threading easier (Fig. 19).

Fig. 19 Adding beads to rings

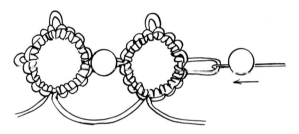

To sew in final ends

Any ends left on completion can be sewn in by overcasting or stab stitching through the heads of the nearest double stitches. If using a thick thread, split the ends into two strands and sew each strand in separately. Both sides of the work should be equally neat, as a finished piece of tatting is usually reversible, without a definite right or wrong side. Since tatting is continually reversed during its production, the front of the rings and the back of the chains will be on the same side.

To save work by preparatory planning

When making a large piece of lace containing chains as well as rings, it is a pity to cut the ball thread in order to replenish the shuttle. Keep a second source of thread for the purpose. This does not necessarily mean buying an extra ball, a supply can be wound onto a spare reel or card beforehand.

   If working a series of repeating motifs, it saves thread as well as work if the exact length can be wound on the shuttle each time. To calculate the amount needed, wind the shuttle with a known length, work the first motif and then measure the thread left unused. The difference between the two amounts is the length required.

Washing and pressing

All tatting will benefit from being damped on completion, as this will shrink the work to a closer tension and make any imperfections less noticeable. If washing is needed, a good soak in a solution of washing powder may be sufficient, or heavily soiled work can be boiled in a saucepan with a watchful eye kept on the proceedings. A robust lace can be machine washed if placed in a pillowcase or similar receptacle for protection.

Tatting should not be allowed to dry in a dishevelled state but should be patted flat with the fingers on a smooth cloth on a flat surface. Any twisted picots can be easily manipulated into position when wet, whereas once dry the task becomes tedious and difficult. If well flattened to an accurate shape while damp, tatting can just be left to dry naturally, and this is often the only treatment needed, especially if the work is beaded. If further pressing is preferred, iron lightly under a cloth. An ornate design may be pinned into position after being patted out flat, the pins being removed only when the tatting is dry.

4 The Patterns

Reading the patterns

The abbreviations used are as follows:

ds   double stitch
hs   half-stitch
p   picot
rw   reverse work

Letters of the alphabet are used to identify particular rings and chains whenever this is necessary to clarify patterns.

Instructions to tie ball and shuttle threads before commencement are omitted as the presence of a chain infers the use of both and, whilst it is convenient for a learner to tie the two threads together in a knot, there are better ways of commencing as tatting skills progress.

Picots are counted in the order in which they were originally worked unless other directions are given.

Patterns marked with a dagger (†) are suggested for beginners.

Edgings

Betsy's Downfall [†]

Using crochet cotton No. 60, the edging measures 2 cm in width.

Ring A of 6 ds, p, (2 ds, p) twice, 6 ds.
* Ring B of 6 ds, join to last picot of ring A, (2 ds, p) four times, 6 ds.
Ring C of 6 ds, join to last picot of ring B, (2 ds, p) twice, 6 ds, rw.
Ring D of 6 ds, p, 4 ds, p, 6 ds.
Ring E of 6 ds, join to last picot of ring D, (4 ds, p) twice, 6 ds.
Ring F of 6 ds, join to last picot of ring E, 4 ds, p, 6 ds, rw.
Ring A of 6 ds, join to last picot of ring C, (2 ds, p) twice, 6 ds.

Repeat from * as required, joining subsequent rings D to preceding
  rings F.

Corner
Work rings A, B and C as before. Work another ring C,
  joining it to preceding ring, work another ring B, joining it to
  preceding ring, work another ring C, joining as before, rw.
Ring D as before.
Ring E of 6 ds, join to previous ring D, 4 ds, join to
  previous ring E, 4 ds, p, 6 ds.
Continue from ring F as before.

Butterflies

Using crochet cotton No. 60, the edging measures 1.75 cm in width and will ease to a curve.

* Ring A of 14 ds, p, 7 ds, p, 7 ds.
Ring B of 7 ds, join to last picot of previous ring, 7 ds, p, 5 ds, p, 2 ds.
Ring C of 2 ds, join to last picot of previous ring, 5 ds, (p, 7 ds) twice.
Ring D of 7 ds, join to last picot of previous ring, 7 ds, p, 14 ds, rw.
Chain A of 8 ds, p, 2 ds, p, 8 ds, join shuttle thread to last picot of ring D, 8 ds, p, 2 ds, p, 8 ds, rw.

Repeat from * joining first picot of ring A to last picot of ring D in all subsequent repeats.

Corner
Rings A, B and C as before.
Ring E of 7 ds, join to last picot of previous ring, 2 ds, (p, 7 ds) twice, rw.
Chain B of 10 ds, join shuttle thread to last picot of previous ring, rw.
Ring F of 7 ds, join to next picot of previous ring, 7 ds, p, 5 ds, p, 2 ds.
Rings C and D as before.
Continue from chain A as before.

Cinderella

Using crochet cotton No. 60, the edging measures 2 cm in width.

Inner row

Ring A of (4 ds, p) three times, 4 ds, rw.
* Chain A of 4 ds, p, 4 ds, rw.
Ring A of 4 ds, join to last picot of previous ring A, (4 ds, p) twice,
  4 ds, rw.
Repeat from * for length required, ending with ring A for corner.

Corner

Chain B of (3 ds, p) four times, 3 ds, rw.
Ring A of 4 ds, join to last picot of previous ring A, 4 ds,
  join to next picot of same ring, 4 ds, p, 4 ds, rw.
Continue with chain A as before.

Outer row

Ring B of 4 ds, p, 4 ds, join to first chain A, 4 ds, p, 4 ds, rw.
* Chain C of (3 ds, p) twice, 3 ds, rw.
Ring B of 4 ds, join to last picot of previous ring B, 4 ds, join to next
  chain A, 4 ds, p, 4 ds, rw.
Repeat from * ending with ring B for corner.

Corner

Chain D of 5 ds, rw.
Ring C of 3 ds, p, 3 ds, join to last picot of previous ring B, (2 ds, p)
  twice, 3 ds, p, 3 ds, rw.
** Chain E of (3 ds, p) three times, 3 ds, rw.
Ring C of 3 ds, p, 3 ds, join to second picot from end of previous ring
  C, (2 ds, p) twice, 3 ds, p, 3 ds, rw.
Repeat from ** three times more.
Chain D of 5 ds, rw.
Ring B of 4 ds, join to second picot from end of previous
  ring C, 4 ds, join to next chain A, 4 ds, p, 4 ds, rw.
Continue from chain C as before.

Cottage Border

Using crochet cotton No. 60, the edging measures 2 cm in width.

Ring A of 7 ds, p, (3 ds, p) twice, 7 ds.
* Ring B of 7 ds, join to last picot of ring A, (2 ds, p) four times, 7 ds.
Ring C as ring B.
Ring D of 7 ds, join to last picot of ring C, (3 ds, p) twice, 7 ds, rw.
Chain of 7 ds, p, 3 ds, p, 5 ds, join shuttle thread to last picot of ring
    D, 9 ds, rw.
Ring A of 7 ds, join to centre picot of ring D, 3 ds, join to junction of
    rings C and D, 3 ds, p, 7 ds.

Repeat from * as required.

Corner

Work two extra rings B for the flower, and join first picot of following
    chain to preceding chain at shuttle thread join.

Daisy Chain

Using crochet cotton No. 60, the edging measures 2 cm in width at
    corner and will ease to a curve.

Ring A of (2 ds, p) five times, 10 ds, rw.
Chain A of (5 ds, p) four times, 5 ds, join shuttle thread to last picot
    of ring A, rw.
* Chain B of 3 ds.
Ring A as before.
Chain A of 5 ds, join to last picot of previous chain A, (5 ds, p) three
    times, 5 ds, join shuttle thread to last picot of previous ring A, rw.

Repeat from * for length required, ending with chain B for corner.

Corner

*Ring B of (2 ds, p) nine times, 2 ds.
Chain B, ring A, chain A and chain B as before.
Repeat from * once more.
(Ring B, chain B) twice.
Ring A as before.
Chain A of 5 ds, join to last picot of previous chain A, 5 ds, join to
    next picot of same chain, (5 ds, p) twice, 5 ds, join shuttle thread to
    last picot of ring A, rw.
(Chain B, ring B, chain B, ring A and chain A) twice.
Continue from chain B as before.

Ewe and Lamb [†]

Using crochet cotton No. 60, the edging measures 1.50 cm in width and will ease to a curve.

Ring A of 4 ds, p, (2 ds, p) six times, 7 ds.
* Ring B of 7 ds, join to last picot of ring A, 2 ds, p, 4 ds, (p, 2 ds) three times.
Take shuttle thread to back of work and tie to third picot from end of same ring.
Ring A of 4 ds, join to next picot of ring B, (2 ds, p) six times, 7 ds.

Repeat from * for length required, ending with Ring A to begin corner.

Corner
Ring of 7 ds, join to last picot of previous ring, (2 ds, p) six times, 7 ds.
Ring B of 7 ds, join to last picot of previous ring, 2 ds, p, 4 ds, (p, 2 ds) three times. Tie to third picot from end of same ring.
Continue from ring A as before.

Faith, Hope and Charity [†]

Using crochet cotton No. 60, the edging measures 1.50 cm in width.

Ring A of (4 ds, p) three times, 4 ds.
* Ring B of 4 ds, join to last picot of ring A, (4 ds, p) twice, 4 ds.
Ring C of 4 ds, join to last picot of ring B, (2 ds, p) seven times, 2 ds.
Take shuttle thread to back of work and tie to junction of rings B and C.
Ring A of 4 ds, join to ring B, (4 ds, p) twice, 4 ds.

Repeat from * for length required, ending with ring C and thread tied ready to begin corner.

Corner
Ring of 4 ds, join to centre picot of ring B, (2 ds, p) seven times, 2 ds.
Tie shuttle thread to junction with ring B.
Ring of 4 ds, join to junction of rings A and B, (4 ds, p) twice, 4 ds.
Continue from ring B as before.

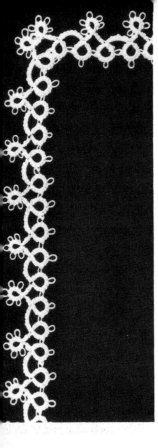

Forget-me-not [†]

Using crochet cotton No. 60 the edging measures 1.50 cm in width.

Ring A of (4 ds, p) three times, 4 ds, rw.
* Chain A of 3 ds.
Ring B of (2 ds, p) five times, 2 ds.
Chain B of 3 ds, rw.
Ring A of 4 ds, join to last picot of previous ring A, (4 ds, p) twice, 4 ds, rw.
Chain C of 8 ds, rw.
Ring A of 4 ds, join to last picot of previous ring A, (4 ds, p) twice, 4 ds, rw.

Repeat from * for length required, ending with ring B to begin corner.

Corner
Chain A, ring B, chain B as before.
Ring A of 4 ds, join to last picot of previous ring A, 4 ds, join to next picot of same ring, 4 ds, p, 4 ds, rw.
Continue from chain C as before.

Hen and Chick [†]

Using crochet cotton No. 60, the edging measures 1.75 cm in width and will ease to a curve.

Ring A of 4 ds, p, 1 ds, p, 5 ds, rw.
* Chain of 8 ds, p, 8 ds, rw.
Ring B of 8 ds, join to last picot of ring A, (2 ds, p) six times, 4 ds.
Ring A of 4 ds, join to last picot of ring B, 1 ds, p, 5 ds, rw.

Repeat from * as required, ending with ring A at corner. Do not reverse work.

Corner
Ring C of 5 ds, join to ring A, (2 ds, p) eight times, 4 ds.
Ring A of 4 ds, join to last picot of ring C, 1 ds, p, 5 ds, rw.
Chain of 8 ds, join to previous chain, 8 ds, rw.
Continue from ring B as before.

Hundred Eyes [†]

Using crochet cotton No. 60, the edging measures 1 cm in width and will ease to a curve.

Ring A of (2 ds, p) nine times, 2 ds.
Take shuttle thread to back of work and tie it to the seventh picot.
Ring B of 2 ds, join to sixth picot of previous ring, (2 ds, p) eight times, 2 ds.
Tie thread to sixth picot.
* Ring C of 2 ds, join to fifth picot of previous ring, (2 ds, p) eight times, 2 ds.
Tie thread to sixth picot.

Repeat from * as required.

Corner

Ring D of 2 ds, join to fifth picot of previous ring, (2 ds, p) ten times, 2 ds. Do not tie thread.
Ring E of 2 ds, join to last picot of previous ring, (2 ds, p) eight times, 2 ds.
Tie thread to sixth picot.
Continue from ring C as before.

Marguerite [†]

Using crochet cotton No. 60, the edging measures 1.25 cm in width and will ease to a curve.

* Ring A of 5 ds, p, 5 ds, rw.
Chain A of 5 ds, p, 5 ds, rw.
Ring B of 3 ds, join to previous ring A, (2 ds, p) eight times, 3 ds, rw.
Chain B of 5 ds, p, 5 ds, rw.
Ring C of 5 ds, join to last picot of ring B, 5 ds.

Repeat from * for length required, ending with ring B at corner. Do not reverse work.

Corner

Work a second ring B of 3 ds, join to last picot of previous ring B, (2 ds, p) eight times, 3 ds, rw.
Continue from chain B as before.

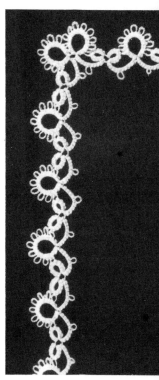

Matthew, Mark, Luke, John

Using crochet cotton No. 60, the edging measures 1.50 cm in width.

Ring A of 6 ds, p, (2 ds, p) six times, 6 ds.
* Ring B of 6 ds, join to last picot of previous ring, 6 ds, p, (2 ds, p) twice, 2 ds.
Take shuttle thread to back of work and tie to third picot from end of same ring.
Ring C of 6 ds, join to junction of rings A and B, 6 ds, p, 6 ds.
Ring D of 6 ds, join to last picot of previous ring, 6 ds, p, (2 ds, p) twice, 2 ds.
Tie shuttle thread to third picot from end of same ring.
Ring A of 6 ds, join to junction of rings C and D, (2 ds, p) six times, 6 ds.

Repeat from * as required, ending with ring A to begin corner.

Corner
Another ring A of 6 ds, join to last picot of previous ring A, (2 ds, p) six times, 6 ds.
Continue from * as before.

Oak and Acorn

Using crochet cotton No. 60, the edging measures 2.50 cm in width at corner.

Ring A of (4 ds, p) three times, 4 ds, rw.
* Chain A of 4 ds, p, 4 ds, rw.
Ring A of 4 ds, join to last picot of previous ring, (4 ds, p) twice, 4 ds, rw
Repeat from * for length required, ending with ring A.

Corner

Chain B of (4 ds, p) twice, 4 ds.
* Ring B of (4 ds, p) three times, 7 ds.
Ring C of 7 ds, p, 7 ds, rw.
Chain C of 7 ds, join to last picot of previous ring A, 9 ds, p, 2 ds, p, 3 ds, rw.
Ring D of 7 ds, join to ring C, 7 ds, rw.
Chain D of 3 ds, p, 2 ds, p, 9 ds, p, 7 ds, rw.
Ring E of 7 ds, join to junction of rings C and D, 7 ds.
Ring F of 7 ds, join to last picot of ring B, (4 ds, p) twice, 4 ds.
Chain E of (4 ds, p) three times, 4 ds.
Repeat from * twice more, joining first two picots of each chain C to preceding chain D as shown. Omit chain E of last repeat.
Chain B as before, rw.
Ring A of 4 ds, join to last picot of chain D, (4 ds, p) twice, 4 ds, rw.
Continue from chain A as before.

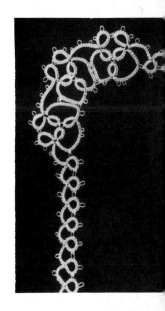

Oranges and Lemons †

Using crochet cotton No. 60, the edging measures 1.50 cm in width and will ease to a curve.

Ring A of (4 ds, p) three times, 4 ds.
* Ring B of 4 ds, join to last picot of previous ring, (4 ds, p) twice, 4 ds, rw.
Chain A of (4 ds, p) twice, 2 ds, (p, 4 ds) twice, rw.
Ring A of 4 ds, p, 4 ds, join to last picot of previous ring, 4 ds, p, 4 ds.

Repeat from * as required, ending with ring B to begin corner.

Corner
Chain B of (4 ds, p) three times, 2 ds, (p, 4 ds) three times, rw.
Ring A of 4 ds, p, 4 ds, join to centre picot of previous ring, 4 ds, p, 4 ds.
Continue from chain A as before.

Ring o' Roses

Using crochet cotton No. 60, the edging measures 3.50 cm in width.

Ring A of (6 ds, p) three times, 6 ds, rw.
* Chain A of 9 ds, p, 3 ds, p, 9 ds.
Ring B of 6 ds, p, (3 ds, p) twice, 6 ds, rw.
Chain B of 4 ds, p, 3 ds, p, 3 ds, join to last picot of ring A, 4 ds, rw.
** Ring B of 6 ds, join to last picot of previous ring B, (3 ds, p) twice,
   6 ds, rw.
Chain B of 4 ds, p, (3 ds, p) twice, 4 ds, rw.
Repeat from ** four more times.
Ring B of 6 ds, join to last picot of previous ring B, 3 ds, p, 3 ds, join
   to first picot of first ring B, 6 ds.
Chain A of 9 ds, p, 3 ds, p, 9 ds, rw.
Ring A of 6 ds, join to first picot of last chain B, (6 ds, p) twice,
   6 ds, rw.

Repeat from * for length required, ending with ring A for corner. Do
   not reverse work.

Corner
Second ring A of 6 ds, join to last picot of previous ring A, (6 ds, p)
   twice, 6 ds, rw.
Chain A of 9 ds, join to last picot of previous chain A, 3 ds, p, 9 ds.
Continue from first ring B as before.

Separate corner motif
Ring B of 6 ds, p, (3 ds, p) twice, 6 ds, rw.
Chain C of 7 ds, join to centre picot of chain B nearest to corner, 7
   ds, rw.
Ring B of 6 ds, join to last picot of previous ring B, (3 ds, p) twice,
   6 ds, rw.
Chain C of 7 ds, join to junction of two corner rings A, 7 ds, rw.
Ring B as before.
Chain C of 7 ds, join to centre picot of next chain B, 7 ds, rw.
Work (ring B, chain B) six times, joining sixth ring B to first ring B to
   complete round. Tie final chain to beginning of round.

Strawberries, Sugar and Cream[†]

Using crochet cotton No. 60, the edging measures 1 cm in width and will ease to a curve.

Ring A of 4 ds, p, 2 ds, p, 4 ds.
* Ring B of 4 ds, join to last picot of ring A, (2 ds, p) seven times, 4 ds.
Ring C of 4 ds, join to last picot of ring B, 2 ds, p, 4 ds.
Space of 0.50 cm.
Ring A of 4 ds, join to last picot of ring C, 2 ds, p, 4 ds.

Repeat from * for length required, ending with ring A to begin corner.

Corner

Ring D of 4 ds, join to last picot of ring A, (2 ds, p) seven times, 7 ds.
Ring E of 7 ds, join to last picot of ring D, (2 ds, p) seven times, 4 ds.
Ring C of 4 ds, join to last picot of ring E, 2 ds, p, 4 ds.
Space of 0.50 cm.
Continue from ring A as before.

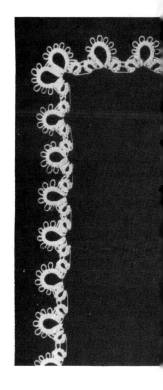

Sweet Pea

Using crochet cotton No. 60, the edging measures 1.50 cm in width and will ease to a curve.

* Ring A of 12 ds, p, 3 ds, p, 7 ds.
Ring B of 7 ds, join to last picot of ring A, 3 ds, p, 10 ds, rw.
Chain of 3 ds, p, (6 ds, p) three times, 5 ds, join shuttle thread to ring B, 3 ds, rw.

Repeat from * as required, joining first picot of each following chain to last picot of its predecessor. End with ring A to begin corner.

Corner

Ring C of 7 ds, join to last picot of previous ring, 4 ds, p, 3 ds, p, 7 ds.
Ring C as before.
Ring B of 7 ds, join to last picot of previous ring, 3 ds, p, 10 ds, rw.
Chain of 3 ds, join to last picot of previous chain, 6 ds, join to next picot of same chain, (6 ds, p) twice, 5 ds, join shuttle thread to last picot of previous ring, 3 ds, rw.
Continue from ring A as before.

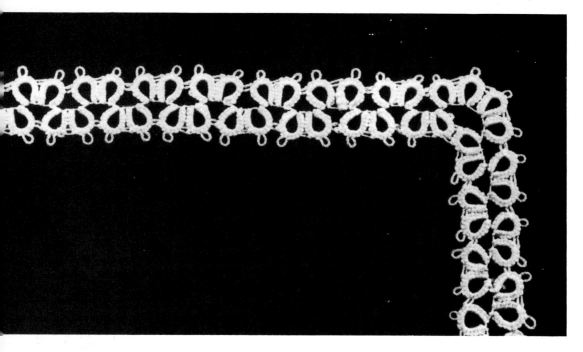

Tears of Love [†]

Using crochet cotton No. 60, the edging measures 1.50 cm in width.

Ring A of 6 ds, p, (3 ds, p) twice, 6 ds.
Ring B of 6 ds, join to last picot of previous ring, (3 ds, p) twice, 6 ds, rw.
Ring C as ring A.
Ring D as ring B, rw.
* Ring A of 6 ds, join to last picot of ring B, (3 ds, p) twice, 6 ds.
Ring B as before.
Ring C of 6 ds, join to last picot of ring D, (3 ds, p) twice, 6 ds.
Ring D as before, rw.

Repeat from * as required.

Corner

Rings A and B as before.
Work a second ring B joining it to first ring B, then work a third ring B joining it to second ring B, rw.
Ring C of 6 ds, join to last picot of previous ring D, 3 ds, join to next picot of same ring, 3 ds, p, 6 ds.
Continue with ring D as before.

Braids and Strips

Blackberries

Using crochet cotton No. 40, the lace measures 3.50 cm at its widest.

First row

Ring A of (1 ds, p) three times, 4 ds, rw.
* Chain A of 3 ds, p, 3 ds, p, 3 ds, rw.
Ring A of 4 ds, join to last picot of previous ring A, (4 ds, p) twice, 4 ds, rw.
Repeat from * once more.
Chain B of 5 ds, rw.
Ring B of 3 ds, p, 3 ds, join to last picot of previous ring A, (2 ds, p) twice, 3 ds, p, 3 ds, rw.
** Chain A as before.
Ring B of 3 ds, p, 3 ds, join to second picot from end of previous ring B, (2 ds, p) twice, 3 ds, p, 3 ds, rw.
Repeat from ** twice more.
Chain B as before.
Ring A of 4 ds, join to second picot from end of previous ring B, (4 ds, p) twice, 4 ds, rw.

Repeat from * for length required.

Second row

As first row but join centre picot of each ring A to corresponding picot of first row.

Black-eyed Susan

Using crochet cotton No. 40, the lace measures 3 cm in width.

Leave a space of 2 mm between all rings when reversing work.

First row

Ring A of 4 ds, p, (2 ds, p) five times, 4 ds, rw.
Ring B of (3 ds, p) twice, 3 ds, rw.
* Ring A of 4 ds, join to last picot of previous ring A, (2 ds, p) five times, 4 ds, rw.
Ring A of 4 ds, join to previous ring B, (2 ds, p) five times, 4 ds, rw.
Ring B of 3 ds, join to last picot of adjacent ring A, 3 ds, p, 3 ds, rw.
Ring A of 4 ds, join to last picot of adjacent ring A, (2 ds, p) five times, 4 ds, rw.
Ring B of 3 ds, join to previous ring B, 3 ds, p, 3 ds, rw.
Ring B of 3 ds, join to last picot of previous ring A, 3 ds, p, 3 ds, rw.
Ring A of 4 ds, join to adjacent ring B, (2 ds, p) five times, 4 ds, rw.
Ring B of 3 ds, join to adjacent ring B, 3 ds, p, 3 ds, rw.

Repeat from * for length required.

Second row

Work as first row, joining first ring A to corresponding ring of first row by two centre picots, and joining all other rings A on same side similarly.

Clover [†]

Using crochet cotton No. 20, the braid measures 2 cm in width and will ease to a curve.

* Ring A of 4 ds, p, 4 ds, p, 4 ds.
Ring B of 4 ds, join to last picot of ring A, 4 ds, p, 4 ds, rw.
Chain A of 20 ds, rw.
Ring C of 8 ds, join to last picot of ring B, 4 ds, p, 4 ds.
Ring D of 4 ds, join to last picot of ring C, 12 ds, p, 4 ds.
Ring E of 4 ds, join to last picot of ring D, 8 ds, p, 4 ds, rw.
Chain B of 10 ds, rw.

Repeat from * but join first picot of every ring A to preceding ring E.

Coronets [†]

Using crochet cotton No. 60, the braid measures 2 cm in width.

First coronet

Ring A of 6 ds, p, (2 ds, p) twice, 6 ds.
Ring B of 6 ds, join to last picot of previous ring, (2 ds, p) twice, 6 ds.
Ring C as ring B.
Ring D of 6 ds, join to last picot of previous ring, (2 ds, p) twice, 6 ds, rw.

Second coronet

As first coronet.

Third coronet

* Ring A of 6 ds, join to last picot of first coronet, (2 ds, p) twice, 6 ds.
Rings B, C and D as before.

Continue from * for length required, joining fourth coronet to second coronet, and so on.

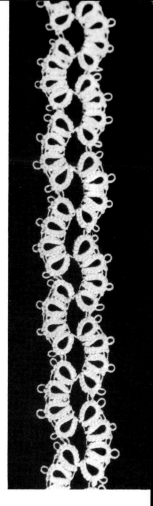

Drunkard's Path

Using crochet cotton No. 20 the braid measures 2 cm in width and will ease to a curve.

Chain A of 1 ds, p, 4 ds, rw.
Chain B of 4 ds, p, 4 ds, join shuttle thread to picot of previous chain, rw.
* (Chain B of 4 ds, p, 4 ds, join shuttle thread to picot of previous chain, rw) twice.
Chain C of 12 ds, p, 4 ds, join shuttle thread to picot of previous chain, rw.

Repeat from * for length required.

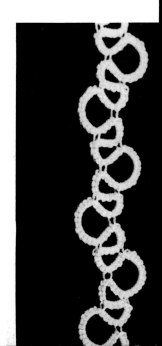

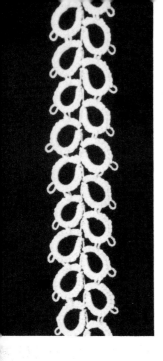

Everlasting Leaves [†]

Using crochet cotton No. 40, the braid measures 1.75 cm in width.

Ring A of 3 ds, p, 8 ds, p, 3 ds, p, 8 ds, rw.
Ring B of 3 ds, p, 8 ds, p, 3 ds, p, 8 ds, rw.
* Ring A of 3 ds, join to last picot of previous ring A, 8 ds, p, 3 ds, p, 8 ds, rw.
Ring B of 3 ds, join to last picot of previous ring B, 8 ds, p, 3 ds, p, 8 ds, rw.

Repeat from * for length required.

Haste-to-the-Wedding

Using crochet cotton No. 60, the lace measures 5 cm in width.

Centre row

* Ring A of 6 ds, p, (3 ds, p) twice, 6 ds, rw.
Chain A of 8 ds, p, 8 ds, rw.
Ring B of 6 ds, join to last picot of previous ring, (3 ds, p) twice, 6 ds, rw.
Repeat chain A and ring B twice more.
Chain B of 4 ds.

Repeat from * for length required, omitting final chain B.

Outer row

* Ring A of 6 ds, p, 3 ds, join to first chain A of centre row, 3 ds, p, 6 ds, rw.

Chain A of 4 ds, p, (3 ds, p) three times, 4 ds, rw.
Ring B of 6 ds, join to last picot of previous ring, 6 ds, p, 6 ds, rw.
Chain A as before.
Ring C of 6 ds, join to ring B, 3 ds, join to next chain A of centre row,
    3 ds, p, 6 ds, rw.
Chain A, ring B, chain A, ring C as before.
Chain B of (3 ds, p) three times, 3 ds, join shuttle thread to centre
    picot of next ring A of centre row.
Chain C of (3 ds, p) three times, 3 ds, miss two rings and join shuttle
    thread to centre picot of following ring.
Chain D of (3 ds, p) three times, 3 ds, rw.
Repeat from * all along.

Work opposite outer row to match.

Heel and Toe [†]

Using crochet cotton No. 40, the lace measures 2.50 cm in width
    and will ease to a curve.

Ring A of 5 ds, p, 5 ds, p, 10 ds, rw.
Chain A of 5 ds, p, 5 ds, rw.
Ring B of 6 ds, join to last picot of ring A, 6 ds.
* Chain B of (5 ds, p) three times, 5 ds, rw.
Ring A of 5 ds, p, 5 ds, join to chain A, 10 ds, rw.
Chain A as before.
Ring B of 6 ds, join to junction of ring A and chain A, 6 ds.

Repeat from * for length required.

Oats and Barley [†]

Using crochet cotton No. 40, the braid measures 1.25 cm in width.

Ring A of 4 ds, p, 4 ds, p, 8 ds, rw.
Ring B of 4 ds, p, 4 ds.
* Ring C of 4 ds, p, 4 ds, p, 8 ds, rw.
Ring D of 4 ds, join to last picot of previous ring A, 4 ds.
Ring A as before.
Ring B of 4 ds, join to last picot of previous ring C, 4 ds.

Repeat from * for length required.

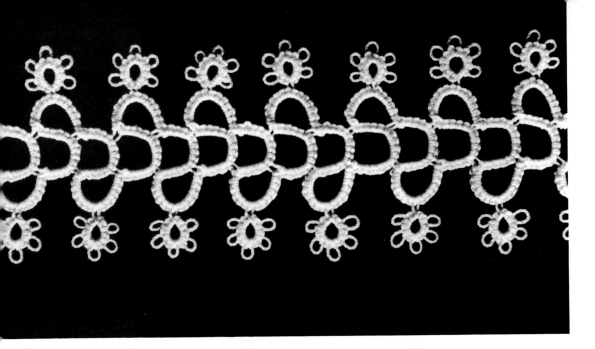

Old Wives' Trail

Using crochet cotton No. 40 and No. 10, the lace measures 3.50 cm in width. Wind No. 10 cotton on the main shuttle and No. 40 cotton on a second shuttle to replace the ball thread.

Using main shuttle, ring A of 10 ds, p, 5 ds, p, 5 ds, rw. Chain A of 7 ds.
Using second shuttle, ring B of (2 ds, p) five times, 2 ds.
Using main shuttle, chain B of 7 ds, join main shuttle thread to last picot of ring A, (5 ds, p) twice, 5 ds, join main shuttle thread to next picot of same ring, rw, 7 ds.
* *Using second shuttle,* ring B as before.
Using main shuttle, chain B of 7 ds, join main shuttle thread to last picot of previous chain, (5 ds, p) twice, 5 ds, join main shuttle thread to next picot of same chain, rw, 7 ds.

Repeat from * for length required.

Queen's Garter

Using crochet cotton No. 40, the lace measures 3.75 cm in width and will ease to a curve.

Ring A of (4 ds, p) five times, 4 ds, rw.
* Chain A of (4 ds, p) three times, 4 ds, rw.
Ring B of 6 ds, join to last picot of ring A, 6 ds, rw.
Chain B as chain A.
Ring C of 6 ds, join to next picot of ring A, 6 ds, rw.

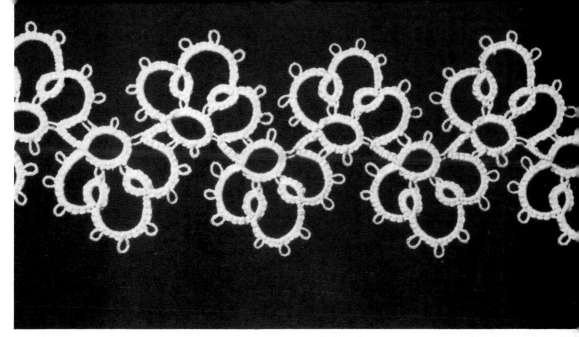

Chain C of (4 ds, p) three times, 4 ds, join shuttle thread to next picot
of ring A, 4 ds.
Ring A of 4 ds, join to last picot of chain C, (4 ds, p) four times,
4 ds, rw.

Repeat from * for length required.

Rook and Crow

Using crochet cotton No. 40, the lace measures 4 cm in width.
Wind the ball thread on a second shuttle.

First row

Using main shuttle, ring A of (7ds, p) three times, 7 ds, rw.
Chain A of 6 ds.

Using second shuttle, ring B of (2 ds, p) five times, 2 ds.

Using main shuttle, chain B of 6 ds, p, 3 ds, rw, 3 ds, join to last picot
of ring A.
* Chain C of (6 ds, p) twice, 3 ds, rw, 3 ds, join to picot of previous
chain B, 6 ds.

Using second shuttle, ring B as before.

Using main shuttle, chain B of 6 ds, p, 3 ds, rw, 3 ds, join to last picot
of previous chain C.

Repeat from * for length required.

Second row

Work as first row, joining second picot of ring A, and first picot of
each chain C to corresponding picots on first row.

Shepherd's Hey [†]

Using crochet cotton No. 20, the braid measures 1.75 cm in width and will ease to a curve.

Ring A of 4 ds, p, 8 ds, p, 4 ds, rw.
Ring B as ring A.
* Chain A of 4 ds, join to last picot of ring A, 8 ds, p, 4 ds, rw.
Ring C of 4 ds, join to last picot of ring B, 8 ds, p, 4 ds, rw.
Ring D of 4 ds, join to chain A, 8 ds, p, 4 ds, rw.
Chain B of 4 ds, join to ring C, 8 ds, p, 4 ds, rw.
Ring A of 4 ds, join to ring D, 8 ds, p, 4 ds, rw.
Ring B of 4 ds, join to chain B, 8 ds, p, 4 ds, rw.

Repeat from * for length required.

Sweet Chestnut [†]

Using crochet cotton No. 40, the braid measures 2 cm in width.

Ring A of (2 ds, p) seven times, 7 ds.
Ring B of 7 ds, join to last picot of ring A, 2 ds, p, 9 ds, rw.
Ring C of (2 ds, p) seven times, 7 ds.
Ring D of 7 ds, join to last picot of ring C, 2 ds, p, 9 ds, rw.
* Ring A of 2 ds, join to last picot of previous ring B, (2 ds, p) six times, 7 ds.
Ring B of 7 ds, join to last picot of previous ring A, 2 ds, p, 9 ds, rw.
Ring C of 2 ds, join to last picot of previous ring D, (2 ds, p) six times, 7 ds.
Ring D of 7 ds, join to last picot of previous ring C, 2 ds, p, 9 ds, rw.

Repeat from * for length required.

Composite Laces

Basket of Eggs

Using crochet cotton No. 10, the motif measures 7.50 cm
  in diameter.

First motif

Ring A of 6 ds, p, 6 ds, rw.
Chain A of 6 ds.
Ring B of (6 ds, p) three times, 6 ds, rw.
Chain B of 6 ds.
Ring C of 6 ds, join to ring A, 3 ds, p, 6 ds, p, 3 ds, p, 6 ds, rw.
Chain C of 6 ds, join to last picot of ring B, 10 ds, rw.
* Ring A of 6 ds, join to last picot of ring C, 6 ds, rw.
Chain A, ring B, chain B as before.
Ring C of 6 ds, join to junction of previous rings A and C, 3 ds, join
   to next picot of ring C, 6 ds, p, 3 ds, p, 6 ds, rw.
Chain C as before.

Repeat from * four times more, joining final ring C to first ring C and
   to junction of first rings A and C.
Tie final chain C to beginning to finish.

Second motif

Work as first motif until first ring B is reached.
Ring B of 6 ds, p, 6 ds, join to first picot of any ring B of first motif,
   6 ds, p, 6 ds, rw.
Chain B, ring C, chain C, ring A and chain A as before.
Ring B of 6 ds, join to second picot of next ring B of first motif,
   (6 ds, p) twice, 6 ds, rw.

Complete second motif as first motif. Motifs are joined on all sides at
   rings B as shown.

Cherry Stones

Using crochet cotton No. 20, the collar measures 6.50 cm in width,
   and the length is adjustable.

First motif

Ring A of (3 ds, p) five times, 3 ds, rw.
Chain A of (4 ds, p) four times, 4 ds, rw.
* Ring B of 3 ds, join to last picot of previous ring, 3 ds, join to next
   picot of previous ring, (3 ds, p) three times, 3 ds, rw.
Chain B of 4 ds, join to last picot of previous chain, (4 ds, p) three
   times, 4 ds, rw.
Repeat from * nine times more, joining final ring to first ring and joining final chain to first chain. For latter join, use the method given in
section entitled 'Special Techniques' for joining a rosette. Tie final
chain to beginning to finish. There should be 11 rings and chains
altogether.

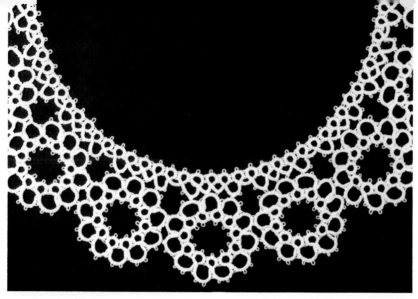

Second motif

Ring A, chain A, ring B as before.

Chain B of 4 ds, join to last picot of previous chain, 4 ds, p, 4 ds, join
to corresponding picot of any chain of first motif, 4 ds, p, 4 ds, rw.
Ring B as before.

Chain B of 4 ds, join to last picot of previous chain. 4 ds, join to
corresponding picot of next chain of first motif, 4 ds, join to next
picot of same chain, 4 ds, p, 4 ds, rw.

Continue with ring B and complete second motif as first motif.

Join a series of nine motifs, or number required, leaving three whole
chains between joins on inner edge, with four whole chains and two
half-chains between joins on outer edge of collar.

Inner edging

This is joined to three chains on inner edge of each motif. With inner
edge uppermost, tie thread at left, to first of these chains, to second
free picot from left.

Chain C of 6 ds.

Ring A as before.

* Chain D of 4 ds, join to next free picot of next chain of same motif,
4 ds, rw.

Ring B as before.

Chain E of 4 ds, join to next picot of same chain, 4 ds, rw.

Ring B as before.

Chain F of 6 ds, join to next free picot of next chain of same motif,
4 ds, p, 4 ds, rw.

Ring B as before.

Chain G of 6 ds, rw.

Ring B as before.

Chain H of 4 ds, p, 4 ds, join to corresponding picot of next chain of
following motif, 6 ds, rw.

Ring B as before.

Repeat from * all along, working end of row to match beginning.

Cloudburst

Using crochet cotton No. 20, the mat measures 23 cm in diameter.

First motif

Ring A of (5 ds, p) five times, 5 ds, rw.
Chain A of (5 ds, p) three times, 5 ds, rw.
* Ring B of 7 ds, join to last picot of ring A, 7 ds, rw.
Chain B as chain A.
Ring C of 7 ds, join to next picot of ring A, 7 ds, rw.
Chain C of (5 ds, p) three times, 5 ds, join shuttle thread to next picot
  of ring A, 7 ds, rw.
Ring A as before.
Chain A of 5 ds, join to last picot of chain C, (5 ds, p) twice, 5 ds, rw.
Repeat from * once more, then work ring B, chain B, ring C, chain
  C and ring A as before.
Chain D of 10 ds, join to last picot of previous chain C, 5 ds, p, 5 ds,
  rw.
Ring B as before.
Chain E of 7 ds, rw.
Ring A, chain A, ring B as before
Chain F of 5 ds, p, 5 ds.
Ring D of 7 ds, p, 7 ds, rw.
Chain G of 5 ds, rw.
Ring E as ring D.
Chain H as chain F.
Ring C and chain C as before.
Ring C of 7 ds, join to next picot of fourth ring A, 7 ds, rw.
Chain I of 5 ds, p, 5 ds, join to first picot of first chain A, using the
  method for joining a rosette, 10 ds, join shuttle thread to next picot
  of fourth ring A, 7 ds.
Tie to base of first ring A to finish.

Second motif

Work as first motif until third ring A has been made.
Chain A and ring B as before.
Chain B of 5 ds, p, 5 ds, join to corresponding picot of
  corresponding chain B of first motif, 5 ds, join to next picot of same
  chain, 5 ds, rw.
Ring C as before.
Chain C of 5 ds, join to corresponding picot of first motif, (5 ds, p)
  twice, 5 ds, join shuttle thread to next picot of ring A, 7 ds, rw.
Continue as first motif until fifth ring A has been worked.
Chain A of 5 ds, p, 5 ds, join to corresponding picot of
corresponding chain C of first motif, 5 ds, join to next picot of same
  chain, 5 ds, rw.
Ring B and chain F as before.

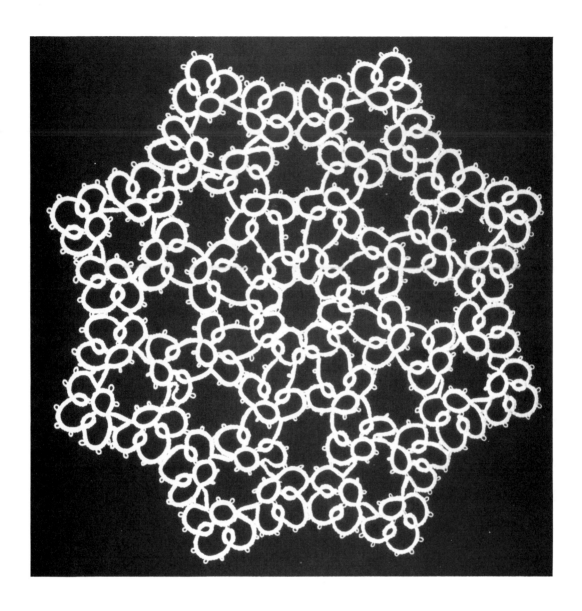

Ring D of 7 ds, join to ring E of first motif, 7 ds, rw.
Complete second motif as first motif.

Work six more motifs, joined in this way, with final motif joined to
  first motif.

Centre filling

Tie to junction of any pair of rings.
Chain of 5 ds, p, 5 ds, p, 5 ds.
* Tie shuttle thread to junction of next pair of rings. Chain of 5 ds,
  join to last picot of previous chain, 5 ds, p, 5 ds.
Repeat from * all round, joining last chain to first chain.

Dahlia

Using crochet cotton No. 20, the mat measures 21 cm in diameter.

Centre

With shuttle attached to ball thread, ring of (3 ds, p) seven times,
3 ds, rw. Tie both threads together to form an eighth false picot.

First round Chain of 5 ds, tie shuttle thread to next picot of ring,
(small picot, chain of 5 ds, tie shuttle thread to next picot of ring)
six times, small picot, chain of 5 ds, tie shuttle thread to false picot.

Second round (Small picot, chain of 7 ds, tie shuttle thread to next
small picot of previous round) eight times.

Third round (Small picot, chain of 9 ds, tie shuttle thread to next
small picot of previous round) eight times.

Fourth round As third round, but work 11 ds for each chain.

Fifth round As third round, but work 13 ds for each chain.

Sixth round As third round, but work 15 ds for each chain.

Seventh round As third round, but work 18 ds for each chain.

Eighth round As third round, but work 21 ds for each chain.

Ninth round (Chain of 10 ds, p, 4 ds, p, 10 ds, tie shuttle thread to
next small picot of previous round) eight times. Cut ends and finish
work after last chain.

Tenth round Ring A of (4 ds, p) twice, 7 ds, rw.
Chain A of 8 ds, join to first picot of any chain of ninth round, 8 ds, rw.
* Ring B of 7 ds, join to last picot of ring A, 7 ds, rw.
Chain B of 8 ds, join to second picot of next chain of ninth round, 8 ds,
rw.
Ring C of 7 ds, join to junction of rings A and B, 4 ds, p, 4 ds.
Chain C of (7 ds, p) twice, 7 ds.
Ring A as before.
Chain A of 8 ds, join to next picot of same chain of ninth round,
8 ds, rw. Repeat from * all round, ending with chain C. Tie to
beginning of round to finish.

Outer motif

Ring A of (4 ds, p) twice, 7 ds, rw.
Chain A of 8 ds, p, 8 ds, rw.
* Ring B of 7 ds, join to last picot of ring A, 7 ds, rw.
Chain B of 8 ds, p, 8 ds, rw.
Ring C of 7 ds, join to junction of rings A and B, 4 ds, p, 4 ds.
Chain C of (7 ds, p) twice, 7 ds.
Ring A as before.
Chain A of 8 ds, join to previous chain B, 8 ds, rw.
Repeat from * twice more.
Ring B, chain B, ring C, as before.
Chain C of 7 ds, p, 7 ds, join to corresponding picot of any chain C
of tenth round, 7 ds.

Ring A of 4 ds, join to corresponding picot of ring C of tenth round, 4 ds, p, 7 ds, rw.

Chain A, ring B, as before.

Chain B of 8 ds, join to first chain A, 8 ds, rw.

Ring C of 7 ds, join to junction of rings A and B, 4 ds, join to corresponding picot of ring A of tenth round, 4 ds.

Chain C of 7 ds, join to corresponding picot of next chain C of tenth round, 7 ds, p, 7 ds. Tie to first ring A to finish motif.

Work seven more outer motifs, joining each to tenth round, and each to previous motif, in the same way. Final motif also joins to first motif to complete the design.

Eightsome Reel

Using crochet cotton No. 10, the motif measures 6.50 cm square.

First motif

Ring A of (4 ds, p) three times, 8 ds.
* Ring B of 7 ds, p, 7 ds, rw.
Chain A of 10 ds, p, 3 ds, p, 7 ds, rw.
Ring C of 7 ds, join to ring B, 7 ds, rw.
Chain B of 7 ds, p, 3 ds, p, 10 ds, rw.
Ring D of 7 ds, join to junction of rings B and C, 7 ds.
Ring E of 8 ds, join to last picot of ring A, (4 ds, p) twice, 4 ds, rw.
Chain C of 8 ds, rw.
Ring A of 4 ds, join to last picot of ring E, 4 ds, join to next picot of
   ring E, 4 ds, p, 8 ds.
Repeat from * twice more.

Ring B, chain A, ring C, chain B, ring D as before.
Ring E of 8 ds, join to previous ring A, 4 ds, join to second picot of
   first ring A, 4 ds, join to first picot of first ring A, 4 ds, rw.
Chain C as before.
Tie to base of first ring to finish.

Second motif

Ring A, ring B, chain A, ring C as first motif.
Chain B of 7 ds, join to corresponding picot of any chain B of first
   motif, 3 ds, join to next picot of same chain, 10 ds, rw.
Ring D, ring E, chain C, ring A, ring B as first motif.
Chain A of 10 ds, join to corresponding picot of next chain A of first
   motif, 3 ds, join to next picot of same chain, 7 ds, rw.

Complete second motif to match first motif, and join successive
   motifs in rows to form an all-over lace.

Fan and Ribbon

Using crochet cotton No. 40, the collar measures 7.50 cm in width, and the length and curvature are adjustable.

Fan motif

With shuttle attached to ball thread, centre ring of (2 ds, p) 13 times, 2 ds. Tie ball and shuttle threads to form a false fourteenth picot.
Chain A of 10 ds, rw.
Ring A of 5 ds, p, 5 ds, rw.
Chain B of 6 ds, rw.
Ring B of 7 ds, p, 7 ds, rw.
* Chain C of (3 ds, p) five times, 3 ds, join shuttle thread to picot of ring B.
Chain D of 6 ds, join shuttle thread to picot of ring A.
Chain E of 10 ds, join shuttle thread to next picot on centre ring. **
Chain A of 10 ds, join in parallel to chain E at junction with ring A, rw.
Ring A as before.
Chain B of 6 ds, join in parallel to chain D, rw.
Ring B as before.
Repeat from * to ** once, thus completing one segment of fan motif.

For second segment, chain A of 10 ds, join in parallel to chain E at junction with ring A, rw.
Ring A as before.
Chain B of 6 ds, rw.
Ring B as before.
Repeat from * to ** once, and complete second segment to match first segment.
Work two more segments similarly. Tie to centre ring to finish.

Second fan motif

Work centre ring and first chain A, ring A, chain B, ring B as before.
Chain C of (3 ds, p) twice, 3 ds, join to corresponding picot on last segment of first fan motif, 3 ds, join to next picot on same fan motif, 3 ds, p, 3ds, and continue with motif as before.

Make a series of nine fan motifs, or number required, joining each by the two picots.

Centre row

This is joined to straight edge of fan motifs at the two picots on chains C and at the centre three picots on centre rings.

Ring A of 7 ds, join to first picot on straight edge of collar, 7 ds, rw.
Chain A of 7 ds, rw.
Ring B of 7 ds, join to next picot along straight edge, 7 ds.
* Ring C of 7 ds, p, 7 ds, rw.

Chain B of 7 ds, p, 7ds.

Ring D as ring C.

Chain C of 7 ds, join to ring C, 7 ds, rw.

Ring E of 7 ds, join to ring D, 7 ds, rw.

Chain D of 7 ds, join to second of the five picots on centre ring of fan motif, 2 ds, join to third picot of centre ring, 2 ds, join to fourth picot of centre ring, 7ds, rw.

Ring F of 7 ds, join to junction of rings D and E, 7 ds, rw.

Chain E of 7 ds, p, 7ds, rw.

Ring G of 7 ds, join to junction of rings D, E and F, 7 ds.

Chain F as chain E.

Ring H of 7 ds, join to chain E, 7 ds.

Ring I of 7 ds, join to next picot along straight edge of fan motif, 7 ds, rw.

Chain G of 7 ds, rw.

Ring J of 7 ds, join to next picot on fan motif, 2 ds, join to nearest picot on next fan motif, 7 ds, rw.

Chain H as chain G.

Ring K of 7 ds, join to next picot on fan motif, 7 ds.

Repeat from * all along collar, finishing end of row to match beginning.

Inner edging

Ring A of 4 ds, p, 4 ds, join to base of first ring of centre row, 4 ds, p, 4 ds, rw.

Chain A of 10 ds.

Ring B of (3 ds, p) three times, 3 ds, rw.

Chain B of 4 ds, rw.

Ring B of 3 ds, join to last picot of previous ring B, (3 ds, p) twice, 3 ds, rw.

Chain A as before.

Ring A of 4 ds, join to last picot on previous ring A, (4 ds, p) twice, 4 ds, rw.

Chain C of 7 ds, rw.

Ring A of 4 ds, join to last picot of previous ring A, 4 ds, join to next picot on centre row, 4 ds, p, 4 ds, rw.

Chain A as before.

Ring B of 3 ds, join to previous ring B, (3 ds, p) twice, 3 ds, rw.

Chain B, ring B, chain A, as before.

Ring A of 4 ds, join to previous ring A, (4 ds, p) twice, 4 ds, rw.

Chain C as before.

Ring A of 4 ds, join to previous ring A, (4 ds, p) twice, 4 ds, rw.

Continue in this way, joining next, and every following third, ring A to centre row.

The inner edging can be threaded with ribbon.

Goodie Two Shoes

Using crochet cotton No. 20, the shoes measure approximately 9 cm in length. Both shoes are alike and the sole is shown separately.

Sole

Ring A of 4 ds, p, 3 ds, p, 2 ds, p, 3 ds, p, 4 ds.
Ring B of 4 ds, join to last picot of previous ring, 3 ds, p, 2 ds, p, 3 ds, p, 4 ds.
Ring C of 4 ds, join to last picot of previous ring, 3 ds, p, 2 ds, p, 3 ds, p, 4 ds, rw. Space of 2 mm.
* Ring D of 5 ds, p, 5 ds, rw. Space of 2 mm.
Ring E of 4 ds, join to last picot of adjacent ring, 3 ds, p, 2 ds, p, 3 ds, p, 4 ds, rw. Space of 2 mm.
Ring F of 5 ds, join to previous ring D, 5 ds, rw. Space of 2 mm.
Ring E as before. Space of 2 mm.

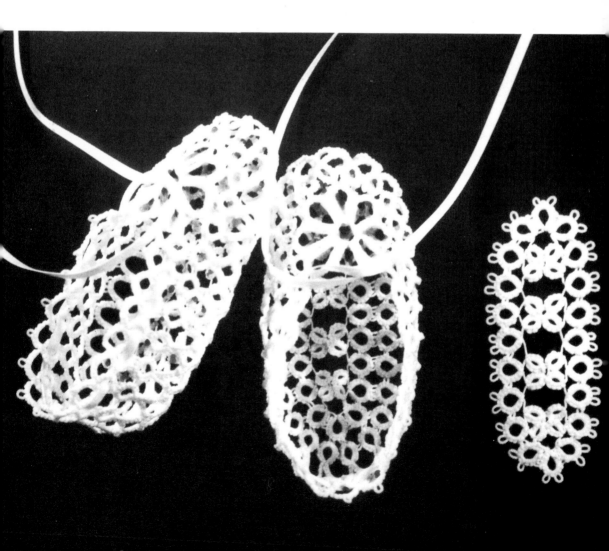

Repeat from * three times more, omitting rw and space after
  last ring E.
Ring B as before.
Ring C as before. Space of 2 mm.
** Ring D of 5 ds, join to junction of next rings D and F, 5 ds, rw.
  Space of 2 mm.
Ring E as before. Space of 2 mm.
Ring F of 5 ds, join to same junction as before, 5 ds, rw. Space of
  2 mm.
Ring E as before. Space of 2 mm.
Repeat from ** twice more.
Ring D as before. Space of 2 mm.
Ring E of 4 ds, join to adjacent ring, 3 ds, p, 2 ds, p, 3 ds, join to first
  picot of ring A, using the method for joining a rosette, 4 ds, rw.
  Space of 2 mm.
Ring F as before. Space of 2 mm.
Tie thread to base of ring A to finish.
Mark free picots on rings A, B and C, from 1 to 6, starting
  from the left.

First round

* Ring A of 4 ds, p, 4 ds, join to picot marked 6 of sole, 4 ds,
  p, 4 ds, rw.
Chain A of 5 ds, p, 2 ds, p, 5 ds, rw.
Ring B of 4 ds, join to last picot of previous ring, 4 ds, join to picot
  marked 5, 4 ds, p, 4 ds, rw.
Chain A as before.
Ring C of 4 ds, join to last picot of previous ring, 4 ds, join to picot
  marked 4, 4 ds, p, 4 ds, rw.
Chain A as before.
Ring D of 4 ds, join to last picot of previous ring, 4 ds, join to picot
  marked 3, 4 ds, p, 4 ds, rw.
Chain A as before.
Ring E of 4 ds, join to last picot of previous ring, 4 ds, join to picot
  marked 2, 4 ds, p, 4 ds, rw.
Chain A as before.
Ring F of 4 ds, join to last picot of previous ring, 4 ds, join to picot
  marked 1, 4 ds, p, 4 ds, rw.
Chain A as before.
** Ring G of 4 ds, join to last picot of previous ring, 3 ds, join to next
  free picot of next ring of sole, 2 ds, join to following picot of same
  ring, 3 ds, p, 4 ds, rw.
Chain A as before.

Repeat from ** six times more, then repeat from * once, joining next
ring A to preceding ring G. Join final ring G to first ring A to complete
round, and tie final chain to base of first ring to finish.

Second round

Ring A of 4 ds, p, 3 ds, p, 2 ds, p, 3 ds, p, 4 ds, rw.

Chain A of 5 ds, join to corresponding picot of any chain of first
  round, 2 ds, join to next picot of same chain, 5 ds, rw.

* Ring B of 4 ds, join to last picot of previous chain, 3 ds, p, 2 ds, p,
  3 ds, p, 4 ds, rw.

Chain A of 5 ds, join to corresponding picot of next chain of first
  round, 2 ds, join to next picot of same chain, 5 ds, rw.

Repeat from * all round, joining last ring to first ring, using the
  method for joining a rosette. Tie last chain to base of first ring to
  finish.

Rosette

This is attached to ten rings at one end of the shoe. Mark free picots
  from 1 to 20, starting from the left.

Ring A of 9 ds, p, 4 ds, p, 2 ds, p, 4 ds, p, 9 ds.

Ring B of 9 ds, join to last picot of previous ring, 4 ds, p, 2 ds, p,
  4 ds, p, 9 ds.

Ring C of 9 ds, join to last picot of previous ring, 4 ds, join to picot
  marked 2, 2 ds, join to picot marked 3, 4 ds, p, 9 ds.

Ring D of 9 ds, join to last picot of previous ring, 4 ds, join to picot
  marked 6, 2 ds, join to picot marked 7, 4 ds, p, 9 ds.

Ring E as ring D but join to picots marked 10 and 11.

Ring F as ring D but join to picots marked 14 and 15.

Ring G as ring D but join to picots marked 18 and 19.

Ring H of 9 ds, join to last picot of previous ring, 4 ds, p, 2 ds, p, 4 ds,
  join to first picot of ring A, 9 ds.

Tie ends to finish.

Edging

Ring A of 4 ds, join to first free picot of ring H of rosette, 3 ds, join to
  corresponding picot of adjacent unmarked ring of second round,
  2 ds, join to next picot of same ring, 3 ds, p, 4 ds, rw.

* Chain A of 4 ds, p, 4 ds, rw.

Ring B of 4 ds, join to last picot of previous ring, 3 ds, join to
  corresponding picot of next ring of second round, 2 ds, join to next
  picot of same ring, 3 ds, p, 4 ds, rw.

Repeat from * all round, joining final ring to ring B of rosette to finish.

Thread ribbon through the rings of the edging as shown, and stitch
  at the back of the heel for safety.

May Queen

Using crochet cotton No. 20, the sprigs measure 5 cm in length, and 22 beaded sprigs are mounted on double net to form a yoke of neck size approximately 45 cm. The depth of tatting in front is 14 cm. To fasten the yoke, use any of the chain loops at the back as button loops.

For each sprig, thread four small beads on the ball thread, and then wind 1.50 m to 2.00 m on the shuttle.

Sprig

Ring A of 5 ds, p, 7 ds.
Ring B of 7 ds, p, 7 ds, rw, slip a bead up to base of rings.
Chain A of 9 ds, p, 5 ds, rw.
Ring C of 4 ds, p, 2 ds, join to ring B, (2 ds, p) four times, 4 ds.
Ring D of 4 ds, join to last picot of ring C, (2 ds, p) six times, 4 ds.
Ring E of 4 ds, join to last picot of ring D, 4 ds, p, (2 ds, p) three times, 4 ds, rw, slip a bead up to base of rings.
Chain B of 9 ds, p, 5 ds, p, (2 ds, p) three times, 5 ds, p, 7 ds, rw.
Ring F of 7 ds, join to last free picot of ring D, 3 ds, p, 4 ds.
Ring G of 4 ds, join to last picot of ring F, 5 ds, p, 9 ds, rw, slip a bead up to base of rings.
Chain C of 9 ds, p, 7 ds, p, 5 ds, rw.
Ring H of 4 ds, join to last picot of ring G, 7 ds, slip a bead up to base of ring. Tie ends to finish.

Work 21 more sprigs similarly.

To make up

Cut a double layer of net to the size and shape required. Damp the tatting and, when dry, arrange 14 sprigs around the back and neck edge of the yoke, with the chains protruding beyond the net, so that the ten front sprigs lie obliquely across the net and pair at the centre front. Arrange two pairs for a second row, then one pair for a third row, and a final pair for the lower point.

Tack the tatting into place on the right side of the work, and then sew it neatly into position from the wrong side.

Attach two lightweight buttons at the back.

No, Nay, Never

Using crochet cotton No. 20, the motif measures 8 cm in diameter.

First motif

Ring A of (4 ds, p) twice, 2 ds, p, 10 ds.
Ring B of 7 ds, p, 7 ds, rw.
Chain A of 7 ds, p, 9 ds, p, 2 ds, p, 3 ds, rw.
* Ring C of 7 ds, join to ring B, 7 ds, rw.
Chain B of 3 ds, p, 2 ds, p, 9 ds, p, 7 ds, rw.
Ring D of 7 ds, join to junction of rings B and C, 7 ds.
Ring E of 10 ds, join to last picot of ring A, 2 ds, (p, 4 ds) twice.
Chain C of 7 ds, p, 7 ds.
Rings A and B as before.
Chain A of 7 ds, join to last picot of chain B, 9 ds, join to next picot of
    same chain, 2 ds, p, 3 ds, rw.

Repeat from * four times more.
Ring C as before.
Chain B of 3 ds, p, 2 ds, join to adjacent picot of first chain A, 9 ds,
    join to next picot of same chain, 7 ds, rw.
Rings D and E, chain C, as before.
Tie to beginning of motif to finish.

Second motif

Work as first motif until ring E is reached.
Ring E of 10 ds, join to last picot of ring A, 2 ds, join to
    corresponding picot of ring A on first motif, 4 ds, join to next picot
    of same ring, 4 ds.
Chain C as before.
Ring A of 4 ds, join to corresponding picot of ring D on first motif,
    4 ds, join to next picot of same ring, 2 ds, p, 10 ds.

Complete second motif as first motif. Motifs are joined on all sides at
    rings A and D as shown.

Pear and Apple

Using crochet cotton No. 20, the motif measures 6.50 cm in diameter.

First motif

Ring A of 4 ds, p, 4 ds, p, 8 ds.
Chain A of 4 ds, rw.
Ring B of (4 ds, p) three times, 4 ds, rw.
Chain B of 6 ds, join to last picot of ring A, (4 ds, p) three times, 6 ds, rw.
* Ring B of 4 ds, join to last picot of previous ring B, (4 ds, p) twice, 4 ds, rw.
Chain C of 4 ds.
Ring C of 8 ds, join to last picot of chain B, 4 ds, p, 4 ds.
Ring A, chain A, as before.
Ring B of 4 ds, join to last picot of previous ring B, (4 ds, p) twice, 4 ds, rw.
Chain B as before.
Repeat from * four more times.
Ring B of 4 ds, join to last picot of previous ring B, 4 ds, p, 4 ds, join to first picot of first ring B, 4 ds, rw.
Chain C, ring C, as before.
Tie to beginning of motif to finish.

Second motif

Work as first motif until first chain B.
Chain B of 6 ds, join to last picot of ring A, 4 ds, p, 4 ds, join to corresponding picot of any chain B of first motif, 4 ds, p, 6 ds, rw.
Ring B, chain C, as before.
Ring C of 8 ds, join to last picot of chain B, 4 ds, join to corresponding ring on first motif, 4ds.
Ring A of 4ds, join to next ring on first motif, 4 ds, p, 8 ds.
Chain A, ring B, as before.
Chain B of 6 ds, join to last picot of ring A, 4 ds, join to corresponding picot of chain B on first motif, (4 ds, p) twice, 6 ds.

Complete remainder of second motif as first motif. Motifs are joined on all sides as shown.

Primrose Path

Using crochet cotton No. 10, the mat measures 23 cm in diameter.

Primrose motif

With shuttle attached to ball thread.

First flower

Ring A of 7 ds, p, (4 ds, p) twice, 7 ds.
Ring B of 7 ds, join to last picot of previous ring, (4 ds, p) twice, 7 ds.
Ring C as ring B.
Ring D as ring B.
Ring E of 7 ds, join to last picot of previous ring, (4 ds, p) twice,
   7 ds, rw.
Chain A of (7 ds, p) twice, 7 ds
Ring F of 6 ds, p, 3 ds, p, 6 ds, rw.
Chain B of 5 ds, join to centre picot of ring E, 5 ds, rw.
Ring G of 6 ds, join to last picot of ring F, 3 ds, p, 6 ds, rw.
Chain C of 5 ds, p, 5 ds, rw.
Ring H of 6 ds, join to ring G, 3 ds, p, 6 ds.
Chain D of (7 ds, p) twice, 7 ds, rw.

Second flower

Ring I of 7 ds, p, 4 ds, join to chain C, 4 ds, p, 7 ds.
Ring J of 7 ds, join to last picot of ring I, 4 ds, join
   to centre picot of ring D, 4 ds, p, 7 ds.
Ring K as ring B.
Ring L as ring B.
Ring M as ring B.
Tie ends to finish motif.

Second primrose motif

First flower as before.
Chain A of 7 ds, p, 7 ds, join to corresponding picot of chain D of first
   motif, 7 ds.
Ring F of 6 ds, join to last picot of ring H of first motif, 3 ds, p, 6 ds, rw.
Complete remainder of motif as before.

Work two more motifs, joining each in the same way, and join last
   motif to first motif to complete centre of mat.

Chain border

First round

Tie thread to centre picot of any ring A.
Chain of 10 ds, tie shuttle thread to centre picot of next ring B.
* Small picot, chain of 10 ds, tie shuttle thread to centre picot of next
   ring C.
Small picot, chain of 10 ds, tie to ring K.
Small picot, chain of 10 ds, tie to ring L.
Small picot, chain of 10 ds, tie to ring M.
Small picot, chain of 10 ds, tie to centre picot of next ring A.
Small picot, chain of 10 ds, tie to ring B.
Repeat from * all round, and tie last chain to beginning of round.

Second round

(Small picot, chain of 12 ds, tie shuttle thread to next small picot of previous round) 24 times.

Third round

(Small picot, chain of 14 ds, tie shuttle thread to next small picot of previous round) 24 times.

Fourth round

(Chain E of 4 ds, p, 8 ds, p, 4 ds, tie shuttle thread to next small picot of previous round, chain F of 16 ds, tie to following small picot of previous round) 12 times.
Tie ends to finish after final chain.

Outer primrose motif

First flower, and chain A as before.
Ring F of 6 ds, join to second picot of any chain E, 3 ds, p, 6 ds, rw.
Chain B, ring G, chain C, as before.
Ring H of 6 ds, join to ring G, 3 ds, join to first picot of chain E, 6 ds.
Chain D as before.
Second flower as before.

Second outer primrose motif

Ring A of 7 ds, join to last picot of previous ring M, 4 ds, join to next picot of same ring, 4 ds, p, 7 ds.
Rings B, C, D and E, as before.
Chain A of 7 ds, join to corresponding picot of previous chain D, 7 ds, join to next picot of same chain, 7 ds.
Ring F of 6 ds, join to second picot of next chain E, 3 ds, p, 6 ds, rw.
Complete remainder of motif as before.

Work ten more primrose motifs, joining similarly, and join final motif to first motif to complete the design.

Princess

Using crochet cotton No. 40, each sprig measures 5.50 cm in length, and 18 sprigs are mounted on double net for a collar 10 cm in width and 40 cm in length. The design can be adapted for a collar of any size or curvature by adjusting the number of sprigs used.

Sprig

Ring A of 9 ds, p, 4 ds, p, 5 ds.
Ring B of 5 ds, join to last picot of previous ring, 4 ds, p, 9 ds, rw.
Chain A of (7 ds, p) twice, 7 ds, rw.
Ring C of 4 ds, (p, 2 ds) twice, join to previous ring, (2 ds, p) three
   times, 4 ds.
Ring D of 4 ds, join to last picot of previous ring, (2 ds, p) five
   times, 4 ds.
Ring E as ring D.
Ring F of 4 ds, join to last picot of previous ring, (2 ds, p) five times,
   4 ds, rw.
Chain B of (7 ds, p) five times, 7 ds, rw.

Ring G of 7 ds, (p, 2 ds) three times, join to third free picot of ring E, (2 ds, p) twice, 7 ds.

Ring H of 7 ds, join to last picot of previous ring, (2 ds, p) five times, 7 ds.

Ring I as ring H.

Ring J of 7 ds, join to last picot of previous ring, (2 ds, p) four times, 5 ds.

Tie ends to finish.

Work 17 more sprigs similarly, or number required.

Edging

* Ring of 8 ds, small p, 8 ds, Tie shuttle thread to picot so that thread lies across back of ring.

Repeat from * until edging measures 40 cm, or length required.

To make up

Cut a double layer of net to shape required for collar. Damp the tatting and, when dry, arrange the sprigs in pairs along the entire outer edge of collar, with two extra sprigs at each end, inside the edging, as shown. Tack the sprigs into place on the right side of the work, and then tack the neck edging also. Sew tatting neatly into position from the wrong side.

Rosette and Ring

Using crochet cotton No. 20, the motif measures 6 cm in diameter.

First motif

Centre rosette

Ring of 8 ds, p, 4 ds, p, 2 ds, p, 4 ds, p, 8 ds.
* Ring of 8 ds, join to last picot of previous ring, 4 ds, p, 2 ds, p, 4 ds, p, 8 ds.
Repeat from * seven times more, joining last ring to first ring to complete rosette. Tie ends but do not cut the thread. Tie shuttle thread to junction of first and last picots where the rosette was joined, then tie to next free picot on outer edge. Leave a space of 3 mm before beginning outer round.

Outer round

Ring A of 2 ds, join to same picot, 2 ds, rw. Space of 3 mm.
Ring B of 6 ds, p, 4 ds, p, 2 ds, p, 4 ds, p, 6 ds, rw. Space of 3 mm.
* Ring A of 2 ds, join to next picot on edge of rosette, 2 ds, rw. Space of 3 mm.
Ring B of 6 ds, join to last picot of previous ring B, 4 ds, p, 2 ds, p, 4 ds, p, 6 ds, rw. Space of 3 mm.
Repeat from * all round, joining first and last rings B using the method for joining a rosette.
Tie to first ring A to finish. There should be 18 rings B.

Second motif

Work as first motif until first ring B.
Ring B of 6 ds, p, 4 ds, join to corresponding picot of any ring B of first motif, 2 ds, join to next picot of same ring, 4 ds, p, 6 ds, rw. Space of 3 mm.
Ring A as before. Space of 3 mm.
Ring B of 6 ds, join to previous ring B, 4 ds, join to corresponding picot of next ring B of first motif, 2 ds, join to next picot of same ring, 4 ds, p, 6 ds, rw. Space of 3 mm.
Complete remainder of second motif as first motif. Motifs are joined on either side by two consecutive rings, leaving one free ring between joins as shown.

Spinning Wheels

Using crochet cotton No. 10, the motif measures 8 cm in diameter.

First motif

Ring A of 7 ds, p, 4 ds, p, 9 ds.

Ring B of 7 ds, p, 7 ds, rw.

Chain A of 7 ds, p, 11 ds, small p, 1 ds, small p, 9 ds, join shuttle
  thread to ring B.

* Chain B of 9 ds, join to last small picot of chain A, 1 ds, small p,
  11 ds, p, 7 ds, rw.

Ring C of 7 ds, join to junction of chains with ring B, 7 ds.

Ring D of 9 ds, join to last picot of ring A, 4 ds, p, 7 ds.

Chain C of 14 ds.

Rings A and B as before.

Chain A of 7 ds, join to last picot of chain B, 11 ds, join to small picot
  of chain B, 1 ds, small p, 9 ds, join shuttle thread to ring B.

Repeat from * four times more.

Chain B as before but join to chain A at beginning of motif.

Rings C and D, chain C, as before.

Tie to beginning of motif to finish.

Second motif

Work as first motif until ring D is reached.

Ring D of 9 ds, join to last picot of ring A, 4 ds, join to corresponding
  picot of any ring A of first motif, 7 ds.

Chain C as before.

Ring A of 7 ds, join to corresponding picot on ring D of first motif,
  4 ds, p, 9 ds.

Complete second motif as first motif. Motifs are joined on all sides
  at rings A and D as shown.

Individual Laces and Fragments

Anemone[†]

Using crochet cotton No. 40, the lace measures 4 cm in length.

Main flower

Ring A of 7 ds, p, (2 ds, p) four times, 9 ds.
Ring B of 9 ds, join to last picot of previous ring, (2 ds, p) four times, 9 ds.
Ring C as ring B.
Ring D as ring B.
Ring E as ring B.
Ring F of 9 ds, join to last picot of ring E, (2 ds, p) four times, 7 ds, rw.
Chain of (9 ds, p) five times, 9 ds, rw.

Half-flower

Ring G of 5 ds, p, (2 ds, p) three times, 7 ds.
Ring H of 7 ds, join to last picot of ring G, (2 ds, p) three times, 7 ds.
Ring I of 7 ds, join to last picot of ring H, 2 ds, join to first free picot of ring F, 2 ds, join to next free picot of ring E, 2 ds, p, 7 ds.
Ring J of 7 ds, join to last picot of ring I, (2 ds, p) three times, 5 ds.
Tie ends to finish.

Flower Fragment [†]

Using crochet cotton No. 40, the lace measures 5 cm in length.

Ring A of 7 ds, p, (2 ds, p) six times, 7 ds.
Ring B of 7 ds, join to last picot of previous ring, (2 ds, p) six times, 7 ds.
Ring C as ring B.
Ring D of 7 ds, join to last picot of previous ring, (2 ds, p) six times, 7 ds, rw.
Chain A of (7 ds, p) twice, 7 ds, rw.
Ring E of 9 ds, p, 6 ds, rw.
Chain B of 10 ds, rw.
Ring F of 6 ds, join to ring E, 2 ds, p, 1 ds, p, 6 ds, rw.
Chain C of 10 ds, rw.
Ring G of 6 ds, join to last picot of ring F, 3 ds, p, 6 ds, rw.
Chain D of 7 ds, p, 14 ds, rw.
Ring H of 7 ds, join to ring G, 4 ds, join to ring F, (2 ds, p) three times, 7 ds.
Ring I of 7 ds, join to last picot of ring H, (2 ds, p) twice, 2 ds, join to third picot of ring D, (2 ds, p) twice, 7 ds.
Ring J of 7 ds, join to last picot of previous ring, (2 ds, p) five times, 7 ds.
Ring K as ring J.
Tie ends to finish.

Josephine Wreath

Using crochet cotton No. 40, the lace measures 5 cm in diameter. A second shuttle is needed for the outer round.

Centre rosette

Ring of 6 ds, p, (2 ds, p) six times, 6 ds.
* Ring of 6 ds, join to last picot of previous ring, (2 ds, p) six
   times, 6ds.
Repeat from * four times more, joining last ring to first ring to
   complete rosette. Tie ends to finish.

Outer round

Wind both shuttles on one continuous thread.
Using main shuttle, ring A of 6 ds, join to second free picot of any
   centre ring, 6 ds.
* Ring B of 6 ds, join to fourth free picot of next centre ring, 6 ds, rw.
Using second shuttle, Josephine knot of 12 hs.
Using main shuttle, chain of 7 ds.
** *Using second shuttle,* ring C of 2 ds, p, (1 ds, p) four times, 2 ds.
Using main shuttle, chain of 7 ds.
Repeat from ** once more, rw.
Ring A of 6 ds, join to second free picot of same centre ring, 6 ds.
Repeat from * all round, ending with a chain. Tie to beginning of
   round to finish.

Looped Sprig[†]

This sprig is intended for a frog or button loop. Using crochet cotton No. 40, the lace measures 4.50 cm in length.

Ring A of 7 ds, p, (2 ds, p) six times, 7 ds.
Ring B of 7 ds, join to last picot of previous ring, (2 ds, p) six times, 7 ds.
Ring C as ring B.
Ring D of 7 ds, join to last picot of previous ring, (2 ds, p) six times, 7 ds, rw.
Chain A of 12 ds, rw.
Ring E of 3 ds, join to last picot of ring D, 2 ds, join to next picot of same ring, (2 ds, p) twice, 5 ds, rw.
Chain B of 20 ds, rw.
Ring F of 5 ds, join to last picot of ring E, 2 ds, join to next picot of same ring, (2 ds, p) twice, 3 ds, rw.
Chain A as before.
Ring G of 7 ds, join to last picot of ring F, 2 ds, join to next picot of same ring, (2 ds, join to next picot of ring D) twice, (2 ds, p) three times, 7 ds.
Work three more rings as ring B, and tie ends to finish.

Note that the length of chain B can be adjusted if necessary to fit a particular button.

Mark-my-Words

Using crochet cotton No. 40, the cross measures 9 cm in height.

Ring A of 9 ds, p, 9 ds, p, 3 ds.
Ring B of 3 ds, join to last picot of previous ring, 6 ds, p, (3 ds, p)
 six times, 6 ds, p, 3 ds.
Ring C of 3 ds, join to last picot of previous ring, 9 ds, p, 9 ds, rw.
Chain A of 9 ds, rw.
Ring D of 9 ds, p, 9 ds, rw.
Chain B of 3 ds, p, 6 ds, p, 3 ds, rw.
Ring E of 9 ds, join to previous ring, 9 ds, rw.

Chain C of 9 ds, rw.
Ring F of 9 ds, p, 9 ds, rw.
Chain D of (3 ds, p) four times, 3 ds, rw.
* Ring G of 9 ds, join to previous ring, 9 ds, p, 3 ds.
Ring H of 3 ds, join to previous ring, 6 ds, p. (3 ds, p) six times, 6 ds, p, 3 ds.
Ring I of 3 ds, join to last picot of previous ring, 9 ds, p, 9 ds, rw.
Chain D of 3 ds, join to last picot of previous chain, (3 ds, p) three times, 3 ds, rw.

Repeat from * twice more, joining last picot of last chain D to first picot of first chain D.
Ring F of 9 ds, join to previous ring, 9 ds, rw.
Chain C and ring D as before.
Chain B of 3 ds, join to last picot of previous chain B, 6 ds, join to first picot of same chain, 3 ds, rw.
Ring E and chain A as before.
Tie to base of trefoil to finish.

Mixed Bouquet

Using crochet cotton No. 60, the lace measures 7 cm in width. Wind the ball thread on a second shuttle.

* *Using main shuttle,* ring A of 5 ds, p, 3 ds, p, 4 ds, rw.
 Chain A of 5 ds, rw.
 Ring B of 4 ds, join to last picot of ring A, 3 ds, p, 5 ds.
 Ring C of 7 ds, p, 7 ds, rw.
 Chain B of 5 ds, p, 10 ds, rw.
 Ring D of 9 ds, join to ring C, 5 ds, p, 4 ds.
 Ring E of 4 ds, join to ring D, 3 ds, p, 7 ds, rw.
 Chain C of 6 ds.
Using second shuttle, Josephine knot of 8 hs.
Using main shuttle, continue chain C with 6 ds.
Using second shuttle, ring F of 7 ds, long p, 7 ds.
Using main shuttle, continue chain C with 6 ds, p, 14 ds, rw.
 Ring G of 4 ds, p, (2 ds, p) three times, 4 ds, p, 4 ds.
 Ring H of 4 ds, join to last picot of ring G, 2 ds, join to ring E, (2 ds, p) five times, 4 ds.
 Ring I of 4 ds, join to last picot of ring H, (2 ds, p) six times, 4 ds, rw.
 Chain D of 14 ds, rw.

Ring J of 7 ds, join to second picot from end of ring I, 7 ds.
Ring K of 7 ds, p, 7 ds.
Ring L of 7 ds, p, 7 ds, rw.
Chain E as chain D.
Ring M of 4 ds, p, 2 ds, join to ring L, (2 ds, p) five times, 4 ds.
Ring N of 4 ds, join to last picot of ring M, (2 ds, p) six times, 4 ds.
Ring O of 4 ds, join to last picot of ring N, 4 ds, p, (2 ds, p) three
  times, 4 ds, rw.
Chain F of 14 ds, join to picot of chain C, 6 ds.
Using second shuttle, ring P of 7 ds, join to ring, F, 7 ds.
Using main shuttle, continue chain F with 6 ds.
Using second shuttle, Josephine knot of 8 hs.
Using main shuttle, continue chain F with 6 ds, rw.
  Ring Q of 7 ds, join to nearest free picot of ring N, 3 ds, p, 4 ds.
  Ring R of 4 ds, join to ring Q, 5 ds, p, 9 ds, rw.
  Chain G of 10 ds, p, 5 ds, rw.
  Ring S of 7 ds, join to ring R, 7 ds.

Repeat from * joining chain B to previous chain G, joining rings F
  and P to central long picot, and joining chain G to previous chain B.
Tie ends to base of first ring to finish.

Peter and Paul

Using crochet cotton No. 40, the cross measures 8 cm in height.

Ring A of 7 ds, p, 7 ds.
Ring B as ring A.
* Ring C of 7 ds, p, 7 ds, rw.
Chain A of 7 ds, p, 7 ds.
Ring D of (5 ds, p) three times, 5 ds, rw.
Chain B of 7 ds, join to ring C, 7 ds, rw.
Ring E of 5 ds, join to last picot of ring D, (5 ds, p) twice, 5 ds.
Chain C as chain A, rw.
Ring A of 7 ds, join to junction of chain B and ring C, 7 ds.
Ring B of 7 ds, join to previous ring B, 7 ds.

Repeat from * twice more.
Ring C of 7 ds, join to first ring A, 7 ds, rw.
Chain A, ring D, chain B, ring E, chain C as before.
Tie chain C to beginning of work to finish.

Lower stem

Ring D as before.
Ring C and chain A as before.
Ring D of 5 ds, p, 5 ds, join to lower picot of any ring E of main cross,
  5 ds, p, 5 ds, rw.
Chain B as before.
Ring E of 5 ds, join to ring D, 5 ds, join to ring D of main cross, 5 ds,
  p, 5 ds.
Chain C and ring A as before.
Ring E as before.
Tie ends to finish.

Pot Pourri

Using crochet cotton No. 40, the lace measures 5.50 cm in diameter.

Centre

* Ring A of 5 ds, p, 3 ds, p, (2 ds, p) twice, 3 ds, p, 7 ds.
Ring B of 7 ds, join to last picot of ring A, 3 ds, p, (2 ds, p) twice,
  3 ds, p, 5 ds, rw. Space of 2 mm.
Josephine knot of 8 hs, rw. Space of 2 mm.
Repeat from * four times more, joining first picot of each ring A to
last picot of preceding ring B. Join final ring B to first ring A using the
method for joining a rosette.
Tie ends to finish after last Josephine knot.

Outer round

Leave a space of 2 mm each time that work is reversed.
Ring C of 4 ds, join to last free picot of any centre ring, 4 ds, rw.
* Ring D of (2 ds, p) three times, 2 ds, rw.
Ring C of 4 ds, join to first free picot of same centre ring, 4 ds, rw.
Ring E of (2 ds, p) seven times, 2 ds, rw.
Ring C of 4 ds, join to last free picot of next centre ring, 4 ds, rw.
Repeat from * all round, ending with ring E.
Tie ends to beginning to finish.

Queen Anne's Lace

Using crochet cotton No. 40, the lace measures 6.50 cm in diameter.

Inner round

Ring A of 4 ds, p, (2 ds, p) twice, 4 ds, rw. Space of 2 mm.
* Ring B of (2 ds, p) three times, 4 ds, (p, 2 ds) three times, rw.
  Space of 2 mm.
Ring A of 4 ds, join to last picot of previous ring A, (2 ds, p) twice,
  4 ds, rw. Space of 2 mm.
Repeat from * eight more times, joining final ring A to first ring A.
Finish with a final ring B and tie ends.

Outer round

Ring C of (2 ds, p) twice, 2 ds, join to fourth picot of any ring B,
  (2 ds, p) twice, 2 ds, rw. Space of 3 mm.
* Ring D of (2 ds, p) five times, 2 ds, rw. Space of 3 mm.
Ring C of (2 ds, p) twice, 2 ds, join to third picot of same ring B,
  (2 ds, p) twice, 2 ds, rw. Space of 3 mm.
Ring D as before. Space of 3 mm.
Ring C of (2 ds, p) twice, 2 ds, join to fourth picot of next ring B,
  (2 ds, p) twice, 2 ds, rw. Space of 3 mm.

Repeat from * all round, ending with a final ring D.
Tie ends to finish.

Read, Mark, Learn

Using crochet cotton No. 40, the lace measures 13 cm in length and 4 cm in width.

Ring A of 4 ds, p, (6 ds, p) twice, 4 ds.

Ring B of 4 ds, join to last picot of previous ring, 4 ds, p, 8 ds, p, 4 ds, p, 4 ds.

Ring C of 4 ds, join to last picot of previous ring, (6 ds, p) twice, 4 ds.

Chain A of 4 ds, join to last picot of previous ring, (4 ds, p) twice, 4 ds.

Ring D of 6 ds, join to last picot of previous chain, (4 ds, p) twice, 6 ds, rw.

Chain B of 4 ds.

Ring E of 6 ds, p, 4 ds, p, (2 ds, p) twice, 4 ds, p, 10 ds, rw.

Chain C of 4 ds, join to last picot of ring D, (4 ds, p) three times, 4 ds, rw.

Ring F of 10 ds, join to last picot of previous ring, 4 ds, join to next picot of same ring, (2 ds, p) twice, 4 ds, p, 6 ds, rw.

Chain D of (4 ds, p) twice, 4 ds, rw.

Ring G of 6 ds, join to last picot of previous ring, 4 ds, join to next picot of same ring, (2 ds, p) twice, 4 ds, p, 10 ds, rw.

Chain E of (4 ds, p) four times, 4 ds, rw.

Ring H as ring F.

Chain F of 4 ds.

Ring I of 6 ds, join to last picot of chain E, (4 ds, p) twice, 6 ds, rw.

Chain B, ring E, as before.

Chain C of 4 ds, join to last picot of ring I, (4 ds, p) three times, 4 ds, rw.

Ring F, chain D, ring G, chain E, ring H, chain F, ring I, as before, but do not rw after ring I.

Chain G of 4 ds, join to last picot of ring I, (4 ds, p) twice, 4 ds.

Ring A of 4 ds, join to last picot of chain G, (6 ds, p) twice, 4 ds.

Ring B, ring C, chain A, as before. Tie shuttle thread to base of adjacent ring I.

Ring D as before.

* Chain B as before.

Ring E of 6 ds, join to last picot of adjacent ring H, 4 ds, join to next picot of same ring, (2 ds, p) twice, 4 ds, p, 10 ds, rw.

Chain C, ring F, chain D, ring G, chain E, as before.

Ring H of 10 ds, join to last picot of previous ring, 4 ds, join to next picot of same ring, 2 ds, p, 2 ds, join to corresponding picot of adjacent ring E, 4 ds, join to next picot of same ring, 6 ds, rw.

Chain F as before. Tie shuttle thread to base of adjacent ring I.

Ring I as before.

Repeat from * once more, but do not rw after last ring I.

Chain G of 4 ds, join to last picot of ring I, 4 ds, p, 4 ds, join to first picot of first ring A at beginning, 4 ds.

Tie to base of ring A to finish. Add tassels at each end if required.

Snowdrift

Using crochet cotton No. 40, the lace measures 6 cm in width.

Half-motif

(All joins are to last picot of any given ring unless otherwise directed.)
Ring A of 6 ds, p, (2 ds, p) twice, 6 ds, rw.
Ring B of 6 ds, p, (2 ds, p) twice, 6 ds.
Ring C of 6 ds, join to previous ring, (2 ds, p) four times, 6 ds.
Ring D of 6 ds, join to previous ring, (2 ds, p) twice, 6 ds, rw.
Ring E of 6 ds, join to ring A, (2 ds, p) twice, 6 ds.
Ring F of 6 ds, join to previous ring, (2 ds, p) twice, 4 ds, p, 6 ds.
Ring G of 6 ds, join to previous ring, 4 ds, p, 6 ds, rw.
Ring H of 6 ds, join to ring D, (2 ds, p) twice, 6 ds.
Ring I as ring C.
Ring J of 6 ds, join to previous ring, (2 ds, p) twice, 6 ds.
Ring K as ring J.
Ring L as ring C.
Ring M as ring D.
Ring N of 6 ds, join to ring G, 4 ds, p, 6 ds.
Ring O of 6 ds, join to ring N, 4 ds, join to next free picot of ring F,
 (2 ds, p) twice, 6 ds.
Ring P as ring D.
Ring Q of 6 ds, join to ring M, (2 ds, p) twice, 6 ds.
Ring R as ring C.
Ring S as ring D.
Ring T of 6 ds, join to ring P, (2 ds, p) twice, 6 ds.
Cut thread and finish.

Work another half-motif, joining ring A to ring T of first half-motif,
 and joining ring T to ring A of first half-motif, as shown.

Tattered Heart

Using crochet cotton No. 40 , the lace measures 4.50 cm in width.

Centre

Ring A of 5 ds, p, (4 ds, p) twice, (2 ds, p) twice, 4 ds, p, 9 ds.

Ring B of 9 ds, join to last picot of ring A, 4 ds, p, (2 ds, p) twice,
4 ds, p, 11 ds.

Ring C of 11 ds, join to last picot of ring B, 5 ds, p (3 ds, p) twice,
5 ds, p, 11 ds.

Ring D of 11 ds, join to last picot of ring C, 4 ds, p, (2 ds, p) twice,
4 ds, p, 9 ds.

Ring E of 9 ds, join to last picot of ring D, 4 ds, p, (2 ds, p) twice,
(4 ds, p) twice, 5 ds.

Tie thread to last picot of ring E and do not cut.

Outer round

Leave a space of 2 mm before and after working each ring and each
Josephine knot.

Josephine knot of 8 hs. Tie thread to first picot of ring A.

Josephine knot of 8 hs, tie to next picot of ring A.

Ring F of (2 ds, p) three times, 2 ds. Tie to next picot of ring A.

Ring G of (2 ds, p) five times, 2 ds. Miss next picot of ring A and tie
to following picot.

Ring H as ring G. Tie to first picot of ring B.

Ring I as ring G. Miss next picot of ring B and tie to following picot.

Ring J of (2 ds, p) seven times, 2 ds. Tie to first picot of ring C.

Ring K of (2 ds, p) nine times, 2 ds. Miss next picot of ring C and tie
to following picot.

Complete opposite side of heart to match, ending with a
Josephine knot.

Tie to beginning of round to finish.

Whirligig

Using crochet cotton No. 40, the lace measures 4.50 cm in diameter.

Ring A of (2 ds, p) seven times, 2 ds, rw.
Chain A of (7 ds, p) twice, 2 ds, small p, 1 ds, rw, 6 ds, p, 7 ds, join
 to last picot of ring A, 5 ds, p, 5 ds.
 * Ring A as before.
 Chain B of 7 ds, p, 7 ds, join to small picot of previous chain, 2 ds,
 small p, 1 ds, rw, 6 ds, p, 7 ds, join to last picot of previous ring, 5
 ds, p, 5 ds.

Repeat from * four times more, joining last chain B to chain A at
 centre of wheel.
Tie ends to base of first ring to finish.

Wild Rose [†]

Using crochet cotton No. 40, the rose measures 3.50 cm
 in diameter.

Ring A of (2 ds, p) twice, 3 ds, p, 1 ds, p, 3 ds, (p, 2 ds) twice, rw.
* Chain of 12 ds, p, 6 ds, join to picot just made, 12 ds, rw.
Ring B of (2 ds, p) twice, 3 ds, join to third picot from end of previous
 ring, 1 ds, p, 3 ds, (p, 2 ds) twice, rw.

Repeat from * three more times, joining last ring to first ring to
 complete round and making a final chain.
Tie ends of chain to base of ring A to finish.

5 How to Use Tatting

On clothing

Fashions revolve, returning in different forms, seen through other eyes, and laces in general reappear again and again throughout the history of costume, sometimes with a bold exhibitionist quality and sometimes with a gentler look.

Tatting adapts easily to the two moods of lace wearing. It can be a rich and heavy encrustation on dress, or a dainty edge fluttering as the wearer moves, and it is worth considering the mood of a garment when choosing a tatting design.

Some patterns are well arrayed with picots while others are more sparingly endowed. It is usually the well-arrayed pattern that looks so pretty and delicate when worked in fine threads. Those with a more sparing sprinkling of picots need the rich texture of heavy threads.

'Hen and Chick' or 'Marguerite', for instance, look lovely worked in No. 40 cotton on semi-transparent fabrics such as georgette or fine lawn. A combination of tatting, pin-tucks and satin ribbon is an old theme, pure Edwardiana, but it is a glamorous juxta-position of textures which will transcribe into modern styles with ease. Tatted edgings are sassy on double-layered frills, at wrist, neck or knee level. Be lavish with tatting. It needs enough scope to work its effect to the full. Too sparse an application may leave a would-be admirer wondering whether one ran out of thread, or impetus.

A wedding veil is usually edged with No. 60 cotton. For an average head veil, cut a circle of net about 1.50 m in diameter. Sometimes, when choosing a design it is difficult to know whether a straight edging will adapt to a curve, and so this information is given with the patterns where applicable. Pompoms, made from a gathered strip of net edged with the same tatting, will make an appropriate matching head decoration (see opposite).

Small fragments such as 'Anemone' or 'Wild Rose' can be sewn at random, or in a personal design, on net or semi-transparent fabrics. The 'May Queen' yoke is intended to be inset into a blouse or dress

Opposite: Wedding veil with 'Marguerite' edging

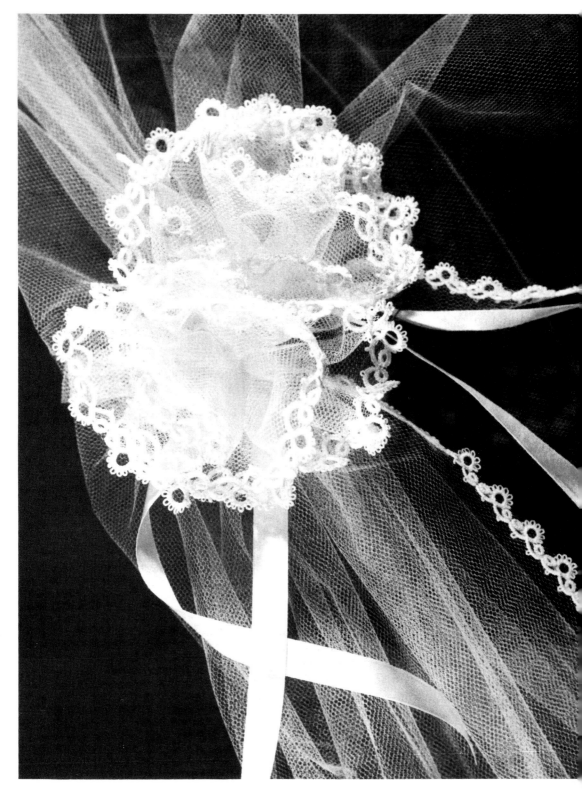

front, and the two lower sprigs can be omitted if a shallower yoke is preferred. Matching cuffs can be made for the collars 'Cherry Stones' and 'Fan and Ribbon' by working shorter lengths of each pattern.

In a heavier mood, braids such as 'Drunkard's Path' or 'Shepherd's Hey' have a sturdy simplicity that will suit heavy fabrics, denim perhaps, or a bold print. Several braids can be used in parallel to build up a wider strip. These two braids are also useful as button loops, if attached so that a row projects over the edge of a garment opening. 'Looped Sprig', designed as a frog fastening, looks especially decorative worked in No. 10 cotton, in black, and used in series on the front of a jacket or caftan (see left).

An unexpected combination of pattern and texture suggestive of smocking can result from applying strips of tatting to gathered fabric, the gathers being prepared in the normal way for smocking. 'Blackberries' can be adapted in this way provided that colours are chosen with care (see opposite).

Other uses

Edgings with a corner design are traditionally valued as handkerchief laces and are still appreciated, even in these days of Kleenex. Handkerchief edgings need to be worked in a fine thread, No. 60, or finer if possible. 'Hundred Eyes' and 'Strawberries, Sugar and Cream' are the quickest-to-work edgings, and 'Daisy Chain' will make a handkerchief for a special occasion—mopping up tears for the bride's mother perhaps. Choose a handkerchief with the narrowest possible hem, for a wide hem can overpower fine tatting. In an ideal world the hem would be hand turned.

The individual designs for bookmarks are obvious, but wide strips of tatting will also make good bookmarks, worked either in black to match the printed text or in a bright colour contrast. 'Black-eyed Susan' and 'Rook and Crow' look very good made up in this way, with fringes at each end.

Uses are self apparent for many of the composite laces. The large circular designs, 'Cloudburst', 'Dahlia' and 'Primrose Path', are intended to be worked in matching sets as table mats, and the repeating motifs are intended for table cloths, large or small, single cloths or matching sets. To make too many identical motifs on the same evening can be slightly soporific, but it does have the advantage that one soon learns the pattern off by heart. Hexagonal motifs, such as 'No, Nay, Never' or 'Spinning Wheels' are especially versatile, as they can be assembled in concentric rounds to produce a large six-sided cloth or assembled in a series of rows as a runner.

Many of the plainer braids make good trimmings for lampshades, especially when beaded. 'Clover', for instance, glints well with drop beads set between the chains, using the method given in the section entitled Special Techniques. 'Anemone' and 'Flower Fragment' were originally intended for mounting in brooch mounts or key fobs,

'Looped Sprigs' used as button loops

for which they need to be minutely worked in sewing cotton. Other individual laces such as 'Pot Pourri' or 'Queen Anne's Lace' are suitable for setting under glass as paper-weights.

These suggestions are only meant to set the imagination working, and most experienced tatters will have no problem in finding ideas of their own for the uses of tatting, although there does not necessarily have to be a use for the product. Why shouldn't one tat as an exercise in cat's cradle therapy, for the creative joy of just making lace—for frivolity?

'Blackberries' on gathered fabric to imitate smocking

91

Appendix

Comparison of metric and imperial measurements
Figures are approximate

Metric (centimetres)	Imperial (inches)	Metric (centimetres)	Imperial (inches)
1	3/8	8	3
1.25	1/2	9	3½
1.50	5/8	10	4
2	3/4	15	6
2.50	1	20	8
3	1¼	25	10
4	1½	40	16
5	2	45	18
6	2¼	100 (1 metre)	40
7	2¾	200 (2 metres)	80

Steel hook sizes
1.50 mm hook corresponds to American size 8.

Bibliography

Works marked with an asterisk (*) contain historical information.

Books on tatting

Attenborough, Bessie M., *The Craft of Tatting,* Bell and Son, 1972.
Auld, Rhoda L., *Tatting,* David and Charles, 1974.*
Benporath, Norma, *Everywoman's Complete Guide to Tatting Illustrated,* Colorgravure Publications, undated.
Blomqvist, Gun and Persson, Elwy, *Tatting: Patterns and Designs,* Van Nostrand Reinhold, 1974
Hoare, K., *Art of Tatting,* 1910.*
Nicholls, Elgiva, *Tatting Techniques,* Mills and Boon, 1976.
Nicholls, Elgiva, *Tatting,* Vista Books, 1962.*
Nicholls, Elgiva, *A New Look in Tatting,* 1959.
Waller, Irene, *Tatting,* Studio Vista, 1974.*

General reference books

Anchor Manual of Needlework, Batsford, 1958.
Beeton's Book of Needlework, Ward, Lock and Tyler, 1870.
Caulfeild, S.F.A., and Saward, B.C., *Dictionary of Needlework,* 1882.
Complete Guide to the Worktable, The Young Ladies Journal, 1884.
Dillmont, Thérèse de, *Encyclopaedia of Needlework,* 1886.
Groves, Sylvia, *The History of Needlework Tools and Accessories,* Hamlyn, 1966.*

Pattern publications (new)

Aunt Ellen, *Tatting Handbook,* Workbasket Magazine, 1982.
Chesno, Helen A., *Tatted Ornaments and Decorations,* 1981.
Chesno, Helen A., *Tatting Made Simple,* 1977.
Chesno, Helen A., *Tatting Patterns Old and New,* 1979.

Festive Tatting, No. 15218, DMC.
Learn Tatting, No. 1088, Coats.
Rice, Adrianne B., *Dillie Delights in Tatting,* Books 1 and 2, 1981.
Tatting, No. 8632, DMC.
Tatting for Today, No. 15209, DMC.
Tatting in Coats Mercer Crochet, No. 919, Coats.
Time for Tatting, No. 813 Coats.
Young, Dora, *All New Knotless Tatting Designs,* 1974.

Pattern publications (out of print)

Learn Tatting, No. 660, Coats.
Learn to Tat, No. 330, Coats.
Orr, Anne, *Tatting,* Book 13, 1918; Book 35, 1935; Book 43, 1942.
Practical Tatting, Weldon's Practical Needlework, Vol. 4, No. 43,
  1889.
Practical Teneriffe Lace and Irish Tatting, Weldon's Practical
  Needlework, Vol. 17, No. 195, 1902.
Tatting, Needlecraft Practical Journal, No. 99, circa 1916
Tatting, Penelope Books 1 to 4, Needlecraft Publications.
Tatting, Spool Cotton Company Books 141, 183, 207 and 229, 1939
  to 1946.
Tatting Designs, No. 380, Coats.
Tatting for Dress and Home, No. 469, Coats.
Ten Tatting Designs, No. 1127, Coats.

Pattern publications (reprints and collections)

Kliot, Jules and Kaethe, *Tatting: Designs from Victorian Lace Craft,*
  'Some Place' Publications, 1978, collection from early 1900s.
Lessons in Tatting, House of White Birches, 1981, undated
  collection.
Old Time Tatting, House of White Birches, 1982, collection from
  1889.
Sanders, Julia E., *Tatting Patterns,* Dover Publications, 1977, reprint
  of Priscilla Book 2, 1915.
Tatting, Books 1 to 6, House of White Birches, 1980 to 1982,
  undated collections.
Weiss, Rita, *Tatting Doilies and Edgings,* Dover Publications, 1980,
  collection from 1920.

Suppliers

General tatting needs

UK

Jo Firth
58 Kent Crescent
Lowtown, Pudsey
W. Yorkshire LS28 9EB

D.J. Hornsby
149 High Street
Burton Latimer
Kettering
Northants NN15 5RL

Jane's Pincushions
Taverham Craft Unit 4
Taverham Nursery Centre
Fir Covert Road
Taverham
Norwich NR8 6HT

Lacecraft Supplies
8 Hillview
Sherington
Bucks MK16 9NJ

Sebalace
Waterloo Mill
Howden Road
Silsden
W. Yorks BD20 0AH

Arthur Sells
Lane Cover
49 Pedley Lane
Clifton, Shefford
Beds SG17 5QT

George White
40 Heath Drive
Boston Spa
W. Yorks LS23 6PB

USA

Susan Bates
212 Middlesex Avenue
Chester
Connecticut 06421

Beggars' Lace
P.O. Box 17263
Denver
Colorado 80217

The Lacemaker
23732-G Bothwell Hwy SE
Bothwell
Washington 98021

Lacis
2150 Stuart Street
Berkeley
California 94703

Craftsman-made shuttles

S.J. Rattenbury (*silver*)
5 Pullman Close
Ramsgate
Kent CT12 6BT

Ian K. Jackson (*wood,
inlaid or plain*)
Old Coach House
Guilsborough
Northants NN6 8PY

Ann Keller (*wood, painted*)
Coolvally
Abingdon Park
Shankill
Co. Dublin
Ireland

A.P. Kingston (*wood,
polished*)
'Erw-Las'
Llanddewi
Llandrindod Wells
Powys LD1 6SE

Nice Things (*wood, flat
notched*)
11 Speke Close
Merriot
Crewkerne
Somerset

Garry Crafts (*horn, flat
notched*)
Tigh Na Car Ruadh
Invergarry
Inverness-shire PH35 4HG

Peter Benjamin
(*Tunbridge Ware*)
11 London Road
Tonbridge
Kent TN10 3AB

Lacis (*silver, horn, shell
and other materials*)
(address above)

Large shuttles
— 4-6 in. (10-15 cm)

D.J. Hornsby
(*address above*)

Lacis
(*address above*)

Tatsy
P.O. Box 1401
Des Plaines
Illinois 60017
USA

Further information

The British College of Lace
21 Hillmorton Road
Rugby
War CV22 5DF

The English Lace School
Oak House
Church Stile
Woodbury
Nr Exeter
Devon EX5 1HP

The Lace Guild
The Hollies
53 Audnam
Stourbridge
W. Midlands DY8 4AE

Ring of Tatters
Miss B. Netherwood
269 Oregon Way
Chaddesden
Derbys DE2 6UR

Index

abbreviations 22
Anemone 73, 88, 90

Basket of Eggs 43-44
beads 18-19
Betsy's Downfall 23
Blackberries 35, 90-91
Black-eyed Susan 36, 90
Butterflies 24

chain 10-12
Cherry Stones 44-45, 90
chiacchierino 6
Cinderella 25
Cloudburst 46-47, 90
Clover 36, 90
Coronets 37
Cottage Border 26

Dahlia 48-49, 90
Daisy Chain 26, 90
double stitch 10-12
Drunkard's Path 37, 90

Eightsome Reel 50-51
Everlasting Leaves 38
Ewe and Lamb 27

Faith, Hope and Charity 27
Fan and Ribbon 52-54, 90
Flower Fragment 74, 90
Forget-me-not 28
frivolité 6

Goodie Two Shoes 55-57

Haste-to-the-Wedding 38-39
Heel and Toe 39
Hen and Chick 28, 88
hooks 7, 92
Hundred Eyes 29, 90

joins 14, 16-17
Josephine knot 6, 18
Josephine Wreath 75

knotting 4

Looped Sprig 76, 90

Marguerite 29, 88-89
Mark-my-words 77-78
Matthew, Mark, Luke, John 30

May Queen 58-59, 88
Mixed Bouquet 78-79

No, Nay, Never 60-61, 90

Oak and Acorn 31
Oats and Barley 39
occhi 6
Old Wives' Trail 40
Oranges and Lemons 31

Pear and Apple 62-63
Peter and Paul 80
picot 12
Pot Pourri 81, 91
Primrose Path 64-66, 90
Princess 67-68

Queen Anne's Lace 5, 82, 91
Queen's Garter 40-41

Read, Mark, Learn 83
ring 12-13, 18
Ring o' Roses 32
Rook and Crow 41, 90
Rosette and Ring 69-70

Schiffchenspitze 6
Shepherd's Hey 42, 90
shuttle lace 4, 6
shuttles 7-8
Snowdrift 84
Spinning Wheels 71-72, 90
Strawberries, Sugar and Cream 33, 90
Sweet Chestnut 42
Sweet Pea 33

Tattered Heart 85
tatting
   derivation 5
   equipment 7-9
   history 5-6
   methods 10-15
   uses 88-91
Tears of Love 34
threads 7-9

washing 19-20
Whirligig 86
Wild Rose 87-88